REJECTION

By the Same Author

How to Overcome a Bad Back
Stop Procrastinating — Do It!

REJECTION

JAMES R. SHERMAN

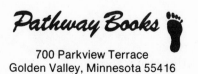

700 Parkview Terrace
Golden Valley, Minnesota 55416

Library of Congress Catalog Number
81-86079

International Standard Book Number
0-935538-02-X

Pathway Books
700 Parkview Terrace
Golden Valley, Minnesota 55416

To: *my amazing friend* Dick Wilson

CONTENTS

PREFACE   ix
ACKNOWLEDGEMENT   x

INTRODUCTION

The Feelings of Rejection   2
A Definition of Rejection   2
A Synopsis of This Book   3

HOW PEOPLE REACT TO REJECTION

Typical Behavior   5
Self-Inflicted Wounds   6
The Key   11

THE CONSEQUENCES OF REJECTION

Frustration and Stress   13
Interpersonal Stress   14
Effects of Stress   15
Wants, Needs, and Desires   18
Defense Against Stress   20

THE CONCEPT OF SELF

Initial Thoughts   23
Your Extended Self   26
Your Inferred Self   29
Your True Self   30
Some Exercises   31

DYNAMICS OF REJECTION

Insensitivity   35
Hazing   36
Balance Theory   38
Depression   41

HOW TO SURVIVE REJECTION

Be Happy   46
Know Yourself   47
Strengthen Your Ego   48
Understand the Process   49
Think of Others   50
Avoid Hostility   51
Disregard the Reasons Why   52
Look for Feedback   54
Look Around You   55
Hang in There   56
Recognize Defeat   57
Reward Yourself   58
Transition   59

HOW TO PROMOTE ACCEPTANCE

Analyze Your Situation   61
Remember Your Past Rejection   63
Keep Your Self-Respect   64
Know What Hurts   65
Insulate Yourself   66
Avoid Frustrations   67
Take Risks   68
Be Flexible   69
Cultivate Your Social Skills   70
Take the Initiative   71
Get Involved With Groups   72
Practice Rejections   73

IN A NUTSHELL

APPENDIX   79
BIBLIOGRAPHY   83
INDEX   85

PREFACE

This is a very unique book. That's because there aren't any other books like it. It's the only one that deals exclusively with rejection. In fact, there are very few books or magazine articles that even mention rejection. It's almost as though rejection is not a major concern, but I know that's not true.

All of us have been rejected more than once. We've been turned down for jobs, had applications refused, and lost out in romance. Rejection affects each of us in different ways, but for most people it causes a lot of psychological pain. Until now, there's been very little information available on how to survive its terrible aftereffects.

I wrote this book to fill an obvious need. I wanted to help people who've been rejected, especially those who feel bad and are unable to find help. I also wanted to discover a way of eliminating the miserable feelings I've had whenever I've been rejected.

While writing this book, I found out that everybody else was reacting the same way I was to being rejected. We were all raising havoc with our physical and mental well-being. Then I figured out how I could overcome my feelings of rejection and be happy again. After that, I set out to discover ways of improving my chances of being accepted in the future. I put the results of my efforts in this book.

Now I know how to survive rejection and promote acceptance. I think it's pretty easy to do. It should be easy for you too. It's just a matter of applying some things you probably already know about. You can do it if you're sincere in wanting to get rid of your feelings of rejection and have more people accept you. Just read this book, do what it says, add to it where you can, and refer to it when you need to. You'll be amazed at how much you can do to make your life a lot happier.

After you've read this book, I'd like you to tell me how well you're dealing with rejection. If you have any comments or suggestions, please feel free to send them along. You can write to me in care of Pathway Books.

JAMES R. SHERMAN, Ph.D.

ACKNOWLEDGEMENTS

Thanks to my wife Merlene and to my sons Chris, Eric, and Lincoln. Their acceptance of my venture into writing and publishing helps me get over the bumps in the road.

INTRODUCTION

You've been rejected. And you feel angry, hurt, and depressed because you think someone turned their back on you. You won't have to put up with that any longer because this book is going to make you feel better again.

Your feelings of rejection could've come from a wide variety of experiences. You might have been turned down for a job you really wanted and thought you'd get. The college of your choice might have rejected your application. The sale you tried to make might have fallen through. An affair of the heart might have left you depressed. Or someone you love might have left you for another. You might even have gone through a devastating divorce.

Whatever happened, it's making you feel rejected. It's a lousy feeling and a very significant feeling. Many psychiatrists think that feelings of rejection are the basis for all serious cases of anxiety and depression. That involves an awful lot of people.

Your feelings of rejection can wreak havoc not only on your emotional state, but on your physical condition as well. They can do much more damage and are far more important than the act itself. Rejection is not a life-threatening event. But your response to it almost always is. Your feelings of rejection are so important that they should be considered before anything else.

THE FEELINGS OF REJECTION

Ever since you've been rejected, you've been experiencing a lot of psychological pain. That's not unusual. Pain is a common feeling that's almost always associated with rejection. If you're like most people, your psychological pain is making you feel depressed.

In addition to your pain, you might also have an intense fear of being left alone. This too is common, especially if you were rejected by someone you love or feel very close to.

You might have lost your self-esteem as the result of a direct hit to your ego. This can make you feel impotent, hurt, sad, offended, bewildered, angry, or bitter. Sometimes you might be so overcome with sadness that you're unable to do anything for yourself.

Your inability to make sense out of your rejection could be causing intense feelings of anxiety. You don't know if you've done something terribly wrong or if the other person just chose not to accept you. You're making up all kinds of plausible explanations just to get rid of your anxious feelings. If your fear of the unknown keeps growing, your world will get to be an insecure and dangerous place for you. You'll eventually lose your normal spontaneity and the confident reality testing that's essential for normal growth and development.

You might feel guilty if you think your rejection is punishment for doing something wrong. Or you could feel embarrassed if you think you were rejected for doing something stupid.

Stress is another natural outcome of your rejection. Excessive stress might already have led to some traumatic changes in your body. If the stress is left untreated, it can lead to serious disease or death.

Whenever you go through an emotional trauma like rejection, it's important to know what's happened to you. Otherwise you won't know what to do to start feeling good again. So the next thing for you to consider is a definition of the phenomenon of rejection.

A DEFINITION OF REJECTION

Rejection is a negative response to an initiated action.

To start with, you offer something to someone else. It can be a product you're trying to sell, an application for a job, an expression of affection, or anything else that means something to you. It could be nothing more than extending your hand in friendship.

Then the other person evaluates your offer. Evaluation is always present in acceptance and rejection, even if it's done subconsciously. It can be a rigorous process that goes on for a long time, or a spontaneous assessment of good or bad. If you run into a lot of psychological problems because of your rejection, it could be due to the way you think the evaluation was made or what you think it was directed to.

Finally, in order for rejection to take place, the other person must deliberately refuse your offer.

Acceptance is the opposite of rejection. The person you offer something to will take it and feel good about doing so. Universal acceptance doesn't exist. Everybody gets rejected sometime. That might be hard for you to believe. But there are lots of good people, including your family, friends, and loved ones, who aren't going to invite you to every social function they have. And no matter what you do, you won't be asked to join every organization or take every job that exists. You can't make every sale because some people will say no and mean it. And you aren't going to hold another person's love if they're going through significant changes in their life that you have no control over.

There might even be times when you want to be rejected. You might want to avoid the military draft. Or you might want to be passed over as a chaperone for a teenage rock concert.

You can create all kinds of problems for yourself if you try to be immune from rejection of any kind. You can avoid the feelings of rejection, but you can't escape from the act of rejection. You'll do much better if you recognize that you can be rejected without prejudice just as you can reject others in a fair and honest manner.

Now you know something about the feelings of rejection, and you have a fairly good understanding of what rejection is. But there are lots more things to absorb before you can start feeling good again. You'll find most of what you need in the pages that follow. Here's a brief description of what lies ahead.

A SYNOPSIS OF THIS BOOK

This book was written to help you overcome your rejection. As you read it, you should be aware of the way it's laid out, because that's an important part of helping you feel good again. For instance, you'll notice that the first section of the book deals with feelings of rejection. That's because those feelings are far more important than the things that happened to you when you were rejected. In the next section, you're given a definition of the process of rejection so you can better understand what really did happen.

Your feelings of rejection cause you to act in ways that can hurt you. So an entire chapter is devoted to the things you could be doing to yourself since you've been turned down. While reading through the examples, you should discover several things about yourself you might not have known earlier. Everyone of them has an effect on the way you feel. At the end of the chapter, you'll find the key to getting rid of your feelings of rejection.

The next chapter tells about some of the harmful things you can do to yourself if you let your feelings of rejection get out of hand. You'll discover the psychological and physiological effects those feelings can have on your well-being. You'll also see how your feelings of rejection get started in the first place.

Another chapter is devoted to your self-concept, which is the single most important element in the process of rejection. Hopefully, you'll see just how important it really is as you read through this part of the book.

Before you learn how to survive rejection, you'll be introduced to some additional thoughts about the experiences you've had. You'll find a chapter that explains how some events can cause feelings of rejection even when you haven't been rejected. A better understanding of those events should dispel the painful feelings you might be having.

Finally, the last two chapters contain specific strategies for surviving rejection and promoting acceptance. The suggestions are clear enough so you can use them right away. But they'll work even better if you've mastered the material in all the previous chapters.

Rejection is a complex phenomenon. It might take more than what's presented here to eliminate all the pain you feel. But with this book in hand, you're on the pathway to a complete and happy recovery. Hopefully, it will be an easy and productive journey.

HOW PEOPLE REACT TO REJECTION

You generally act according to the way you feel. If you think you've been rejected and feel bad because of it, you'll probably respond the way lots of other people do. That's what this chapter is all about. It tries to point out to you the things that most people do when they feel they've been rejected. The reactions are described with you in mind, not as innocuous case studies that you'd have a hard time relating to. When you see yourself behaving in the ways that are described here, it should make you want to change. It should also give you an indication of how you can start feeling better.

This chapter starts out with some commonly observed first reactions. Then it explains some of the self-injurious things you can do when you turn your feelings of rejection against yourself. The last section in this chapter tells how to get rid of your feelings of rejection.

Now, here's a discussion of some of the things you can do when someone else chooses not to accept you.

TYPICAL BEHAVIOR

Most people feel bad right after they've been rejected. They also tend to engage in typical, and sometimes inappropriate, behavior. Here are some characteristic first responses. See how many of them apply to you.

1. **I Did It.** You take the blame for failing to win approval. If you've got a weak self-concept, or if you're unable to come up with a logical reason why you weren't accepted, you'll experience a lot of anxiety and a loss of self-esteem. Otherwise you'll accept your rejection as another of life's many misfortunes.
2. **They Did It.** You put the blame on the one who did the rejecting. You accuse them of faulty judgment and deny your own shortcomings. You're angry and hostile and feel a need to retaliate against the person who rejected you.
3. **It Didn't Happen.** You deny that rejection actually took place. You isolate yourself from the facts in order to escape the pain of not being accepted. You try to protect yourself from an unpleasant reality by refusing to perceive or face it. You'll use some kind of an escape technique, like getting sick or directing attention to other things, so you can hide from your misfortune.
4. **It's Not Fair.** You claim to have been deceived by misinformation, misrepresentation, and a lack of fair play. The target of your wrath is anyone but yourself, because you see everyone else as being against you.
5. **It's Nobody's Fault.** You don't blame anybody. You explain your rejection in a rational way that justifies the actions of everyone involved. You're able to reconcile contradictory judgments by pointing out all the different sides to the issue. If you do all this, you're a pretty levelheaded person.

After the first wave of feelings has gone by, you're going to start thinking more about yourself. But you'll end up causing problems instead of preventing them as the next section explains.

SELF-INFLICTED WOUNDS

You react to rejection in many different ways. Sometimes you're extremely upset, while at other times you're only mildly disturbed. But in almost every case, you turn your feelings of rejection against yourself.

You might find it hard to believe that you're the cause of your bad feelings, especially if you're really mad at the person who rejected you.

You want to blame them for all the bad things that happen to you, including the emotional pain and anguish you're suffering. But you've got to believe it, or you'll never get rid of your feelings of rejection. No one else can get inside you and create your emotions. You do that yourself. You respond to the things other people do to you. If you feel bad, it's because you made yourself feel that way in response to something someone else did. And if you want to feel good again, you have to start treating yourself a lot better.

Sometimes your feelings of rejection are self-serving. You express them openly to try to gain sympathy or support. They usually bear little resemblance to what really happened, and they seldom reflect the feelings of others. When they're self-inflicted like this, they usually represent a significant change in your behavior.

You don't always turn your feelings of rejection inward for self-serving reasons. Sometimes it's really hard to figure out why you do it. Perhaps you just don't know what else to do. But in any event, the effects are clear. You make yourself miserable.

The following paragraphs describe some of the things you can do to yourself when you feel rejected. Many of them are relatively minor. Others can be life-threatening. Study each of them as they're presented and see if they reflect the way you've reacted to rejection. If you can relate to any of them, it should give you some good clues on how to start feeling good again.

Self-Abandonment. Your feelings of rejection have led to self-abandonment. You've given up on yourself, lost your self-control, and are submitting to disreputable emotions, impulses, and desires. You've cast aside your self-concept and are engaged in all kinds of objectionable or harmful behavior with no remorse for what you're doing. You felt abandoned when you were rejected, now you've accepted that feeling as a way of life.

Self-Abuse. If you hate yourself for seeking approval in the first place, you've turned to self-abuse. You get excessively drunk, deliberately overexert yourself, or otherwise engage in physical maltreatment for doing something that you now think was very stupid. You blame yourself for not being accepted. And your anger and frustration are expressed in the harsh and injurious behavior you now force upon yourself.

Self-Accusation. You've resorted to self-accusation if you systematically blame yourself for your rejection. You go over the whole experience of approval-seeking and call yourself to account for everything you did. You accuse yourself of doing something so wrong that rejection was inevitable. If you could, you'd indict yourself for a criminal act.

Self-Annihilation. Your rejection has led to self-annihilation. You've reduced your self-concept to absolute zero. You consider it to be of no consequence in a world you now perceive in a mystical or spiritual sense. You feel the events surrounding your rejection have spiritual or occult significance and are beyond ordinary human knowledge. In destroying your self-concept, you've come to believe that everything is controlled by God or some other spiritual force. As far as you're concerned, there is no self and your destiny is totally out of your hands.

Self-Betrayal. You feel self-betrayed if you've revealed your personal thoughts, emotions, and attitudes to the one who rejected you. You feel you've violated your own confidence by disclosing things you now think should've been kept to yourself. You're embarrassed by what you've done without really knowing whether it affected your rejection or not.

Self-Condemnation. Trying to be objective while analyzing your rejection doesn't always make things better. You're experiencing self-condemnation when you weigh all the evidence and then declare without reservation that you're a reprehensible person. You think you're guilty of doing something so unpardonable that it's resulted in total rejection. You broadcast your pronouncement of guilt to family and friends because of your masochistic desire for more punishment.

Self-Criticism. You're self-critical if you keep stressing your faults and shortcomings, especially those you think caused your rejection. Your persistent criticism is directed to a growing number of personal characteristics that keep coming to mind as you dwell on your perceived misfortune. The more you think about being rejected, the more critical you are toward yourself. You seem to find some perverse pleasure in tearing yourself down.

Self-Deception. Rejection can also lead to self-deception. You see the approval-seeking events in an entirely different way than others do.

Your misperceptions of what really happened have led you to believe things that just aren't true. You're becoming a hypocrite by trying to display virtues and personal qualities you don't have. You do that because you think those things are necessary for acceptance. You're unable to accept the fact that you've been rejected. And you'll do, say, or believe anything that you think will put you at an advantage in the future.

Self-Defeat. You're engaging in self-defeating behavior when you predict or assume rejection before it actually happens. Everything you say or do makes it obvious that you think you're going to be rejected, just like you've been in the past. Those whose acceptance you seek will keep rejecting you because they think you expect it. You live by a self-fulfilling prophecy. And you'll continue to be rejected as long as you believe your goals and objectives will never be met.

Self-Denial. Because your rejection has made you feel guilty, you think you should never have sought acceptance in the first place. Your guilt persists even though you were responding to a basic need. Now you believe that gratification-seeking is bad because it leads to rejection. You discipline yourself by resorting to self-denial. You refuse to consider any need or desire as being essential. You choose to live a spartan life because you don't want to be rejected again. And worst of all, you won't even allow yourself to be happy.

Self-Despair. Rejection can also bring on feelings of self-despair. You feel so hopeless that you don't expect to feel good or be successful no matter what you do. You lack confidence in yourself and in your attempts to gain acceptance. If you're obligated to keep trying, you do so mechanically, knowing all the time that you won't succeed. And if you have no incentive to keep going, your feelings of despair will prevent you from doing anything at all.

Self-Destruction. Your sense of guilt at having been rejected is so intense that it leads to self-destructive behavior. You seriously consider suicide as the only way to make amends for doing what you think was a very dumb thing. To you, suicide is the ultimate form of punishment. If you're angry with the person who rejected you, you'll consider it as a way of getting even. In either case, you're considering an extreme form of behavior in response to some very strong emotions.

Self-Doubt. Rejection has caused you to lose faith in your ability to gain acceptance. A gnawing sense of self-doubt lies behind everything you do. But even though your self-confidence is gone and you doubt if you'll succeed, your need for acceptance is still strong. So you continue to strive for acceptance even though you don't expect much for your efforts.

Self-Effacement. Your unsuccessful attempts at being accepted have led to self-effacement. You've become extremely shy and reserved. You feel comfortable staying in the background and being unnoticed. As long as you're inconspicuous, you know you won't have to worry about being rejected because nobody will notice you. And you're not about to extend yourself to someone else if there's a possibility of not being accepted.

Self-Humiliation. Feelings of inferiority, guilt, or shame have led to self-humiliation. You're so embarrassed over being rejected that your sense of pride, prestige, and self-respect is lost or seriously impaired. You're mortified to think you could've done something so stupid as to seek acceptance and then be rejected. You try to hide your embarrassment by withdrawing from any situations in which the possibility of rejection exists.

Self-Justification. Rejection has led to self-justification. You can come up with an unlimited number of reasons why it was in your best interest to seek acceptance. You can give all kinds of excuses to cover up any shortcomings that might have caused your rejection. You'll persist in stating your case in an attempt to convince others that your reactions were justified and rejection was unfair.

Self-Pity. Your rejection has caused you to turn to self-pity. You dwell excessively on the sorrow and misfortune you're experiencing as a result of your rejection. You'll continue to harp on your tragedy without restraint, because self-pity gratifies your need for solace and comfort. The more you do it, the better you think you feel. Unfortunately, you're totally oblivious to the feelings of those who have to listen to you.

Self-Punishment. This is a common byproduct of rejection. Tremendous feelings of guilt cause you to severely discipline or torment yourself as penance for being rejected. Your punishment takes on several forms, ranging from physical abuse to the nongratification of basic needs. You starve yourself, refuse the company of friends, take unnatural risks, or otherwise introduce chaos into your everyday living. You'll continue this behavior until you feel you've paid the price for being rejected.

Self-Renunciation. You've turned to self-renunciation if your rejection made you give up on your goals and objectives. You've probably cast aside as unacceptable all your desires, aspirations, and ambitions related to those goals and objectives. Whatever it was you wanted to do or be has gone by the boards. You gave up on yourself because you're mad. It's not because of an objective analysis of your goals and objectives. And it probably has nothing to do with the reasons for your rejection.

Self-Repression. Fear of future rejections has led to self-repression. You keep all thoughts, wishes, and feelings inside yourself and don't let anything out. You feel other people won't have a reason for rejecting you if you can completely insulate yourself from them. You don't alter any personal characteristics, you just don't let anybody see them. You remember your past rejections, and you're not going to do or say anything that will cause you to be rejected again.

Self-Righteousness. Rejection has led to self-righteousness. You've become narrow-mindedly moralistic and convinced of your own virtuous behavior. You compare your commendable performance with the implied transgressions and evil thoughts of those who are responsible for your feelings of rejection. If your lack of acceptance has been particularly painful, you probably consider yourself a terrific candidate for martyrdom.

Can you find yourself in any of these self-injurious patterns of behavior? Are there several of them that apply to the way you've been treating yourself?

If the answers are yes, then you should have a real good idea of how you can get rid of your feelings of rejection. Here's how.

THE KEY

The key to getting rid of your feelings of rejection is very simple.

STOP HURTING YOURSELF!

That shouldn't be so hard. But it seems to be for lots of people. Even you might think it's hard to do.

You can't get hurt just by being rejected. There's nothing in the act itself that can possibly bring on the feelings you're experiencing. But you can be physically and mentally devastated by the feelings of rejection and self-injurious behavior that you create and turn against yourself. You can very easily get rid of those lousy feelings by developing a strong self-concept that can withstand any and all attacks you make against it.

You obviously can react to your rejection in many more ways than are presented here. But in general, you're the one who's responsible for all those terrible feelings that keep tearing you up. Even feelings like anger and bitterness that you direct toward the person who rejected you can hurt you a whole lot more. This self-inflicted havoc can ruin your appetite, raise your blood pressure, keep you awake at night, wreck your health, and steal your happiness.

Accept the fact that the physical and mental pain and anguish you're experiencing is self-inflicted, and you've taken a giant step toward overcoming your feelings of rejection. If you allow those feelings to continue, they'll lead you into a whole parcel of physical and mental problems that will be difficult to deal with. Many of these problems are discussed in the next chapter. But before you go on to them, stop a minute and consider the things that are happening to you.

You're letting an event that you might not have been able to control cause all kinds of emotional disruption. You're attacking yourself for being someone that somebody else—for whatever reason—chose not to accept. You're not only generating the problems, but you're also dumping them on yourself. That doesn't make sense, does it? Just think about it for a minute. Then go on to the next chapter and read about some of the other things you can do to yourself. And don't skip anything, because the more you know about your feelings of rejection and what they can do to you, the easier it will be to get rid of them.

THE CONSEQUENCES OF REJECTION

Being rejected is a very traumatic experience. You can not only be emotionally upset, but physically disturbed as well. Up to a point, these are normal reactions. But if you allow them to get out of hand, you'll be in for some real trouble.

Unfortunately, there's no well-defined point where a little bell rings and tells you that you've gone too far. You have to know and be able to recognize the danger signs and either back up or not go down the road at all.

This chapter tells what happens when you let your feelings of rejection go unchecked. It describes the kind of frustration and stress that naturally follow rejection. It tells about the effects that stress can have on your body if it's allowed to continue. Then it describes the things that make you seek acceptance in the first place. It ends with a discussion of some of the steps you can take to protect yourself against the effects of negative stress.

FRUSTRATION AND STRESS

When you were rejected you probably felt frustrated before you felt anything else. That's because you were unable to satisfy your basic need for being accepted. Some barriers came between you and a favorable response. It could've been a physical, psychological, biological, economic, or cultural barrier. But whatever it was, it kept you from getting something you really wanted.

At first, your frustration made you feel confused, annoyed, angry,

13

disappointed, or defeated. If you let it continue, your frustration probably contributed to the initial stages of an anxiety reaction. And until you can identify the cause of your frustration, your anxiety will continue to build to dangerous levels.

Prolonged frustration causes stress. Dr. Hans Selye, Professor and Director of the Institute of Experimental Medicine and Surgery in the University of Montreal, defines stress as "any action or situation that places special physical or psychological demands upon a person; anything that can unbalance a person's equilibrium." It doesn't make any difference whether the cause of your stress is pleasant or unpleasant. What is important is the intensity of the demand for your body to adjust and adapt to the stressful situation. Your body needs a certain amount of stress to keep up its normal functions. But unpleasant stress—called distress—is bad, and it can cause very serious problems.

The frustration of basic needs, like the need for acceptance, causes as much distress as anything. The stress that results from rejection causes mental tension, feelings of insecurity, and aimlessness. These conditions lead to migraine headache, peptic ulcers, heart attacks, hypertension, mental disease, suicide, or just plain unhappiness. The connection between frustration and stress is well documented. The combined effects are devastating.

Interpersonal stress is the kind that's generated between you and another person. It's the basis for most of the problems that come from being rejected.

INTERPERSONAL STRESS

Any interaction between you and another person will produce some stress on your body. That's because your body must adapt to the situational demands that are placed upon it. It makes no difference what the demands are, because the stress can be either positive or negative.

Positive stress builds friendship, gratitude, goodwill, and love. It exists when two people accept each other.

Rejection produces negative stress. It can bring on feelings of hatred and frustration or an urge for revenge, either toward yourself or the person who rejected you. Negative feelings that you direct toward yourself are usually expressed by guilt or embarrassment.

The positive or negative feelings you hold toward others create stress that will either help you or hurt you. The same is true of the positive or negative feelings that are directed to you from someone else. The effects these feelings cause can be either psychological or physical.

Your state of equilibrium and security in society is best ensured when you receive positive feelings from as many people as possible. Negative feelings threaten your security and cause you to be aggressive, defensive, or hostile toward others. Feelings of indifference allow for peaceful coexistence, but that's about all.

Dr. Selye feels that the "incitement of positive, negative, or indifferent feelings for one person toward another is the most important factor governing behavior in everyday life." He thinks these feelings are chiefly responsible for your anxieties or peace of mind, your sense of security or insecurity, or your personal fulfillment or frustration. In short, these feelings determine how successful you'll be in enjoying life's challenging stress without suffering distress.

You experienced a lot of negative stress when you were rejected. But the person who rejected you might have gone through some of the same feelings. That would be especially true if your rejection was affected by guilt, jealousy, envy, or prejudice. In any event, the effects of negative stress were bad for both of you.

The effects of stress are always more important than the events that cause them. That's because stress has a life-or-death impact. And there are very few stress-provoking events that have that much influence.

EFFECTS OF STRESS

Negative stress hurts everybody. If you're particularly susceptible to stress of any kind, you'll have a lot more problems than someone who's relatively immune. The significance of the stimulus also affects the amount of stress you feel. This is especially true with something like rejection, which causes tremendous amounts of negative stress. And negative stress will always affect you more than positive stress.

Negative stress not only affects your state of mind, but your body as well. When you're in a stressful situation, your autonomic nervous system and your pituitary glands reinforce each other to produce powerful and unmistakable signals of stress. At the same time they work to balance each other to keep your body from going out of control.

The extent to which you respond to stress depends on what sets it off. Your general response is like everybody else's. Your muscles get tense and tighten on commands from your autonomic nervous system. You breathe deeper and faster. Your heart rate increases, blood vessels constrict, and your blood pressure goes up. The blood vessels just under your skin almost close to protect you against attack. The muscles in your face contort to show expressions of rage, anger, hate, sorrow, or fear. The muscles in your stomach and intestines halt digestion. And the muscles controlling your bladder and bowels loosen up.

There are other changes. Your respiration increases. Your mouth feels dry because your secretion of saliva and mucus decreases. The perception of your sense organs sharpens so you can hear, see, and smell better.

Your adrenal glands release hormones that cause a feeling of giddy exhuberance mixed with anxiety. These same hormones cause an increase in your heart rate and make your blood pressure go up.

These are all normal reactions to stress. The extent to which they're evident will vary from person to person. If the stress is allowed to build, or if you can't adapt to negative stress, the cumulative effects will kill you. So your ability to survive the traumas of negative stress depends on your ability to come up with ingenious ways of adapting to it.

Dr. James P. Henry, professor of physiology at the University of Southern California, has developed a two-part theory of what happens to your body when you experience negative stress. In the first part, according to Dr. Henry, passive emotions like grief, despair, and feelings of loss or failure are registered in the part of your brain called the hippocampus. When that happens, the hippocampus activates the pituitary and adrenal glands. Your feelings of rejection cause an excessive secretion of hormones like cortisol. If this goes on too long, your body's metabolism gets all screwed up. You lose your immunity against diseases and tumors and your body starts to attack itself. That's when problems like rheumatoid arthritis are likely to develop.

The other part of Dr. Henry's theory deals with aggressive emotions like anger, impatience, and frustration. These affect another part of the brain called the amygdala. Impulses from the amagydala cause secretion of hormones known as catecholamines. These chemicals increase your heart rate, elevate your blood pressure, and raise the level of free fatty acids in your blood. When you're threatened by some danger, these responses are normal. But if they're allowed to persist, you'll develop migraine headaches, hypertension, coronary heart disease, strokes, or other disabilities.

According to Dr. Henry, if you can't cope with frustration and negative stress, you're going to experience serious physiological problems no matter how you react. His research indicates that a person's ability to cope is "enormously dependent on the person's self-esteem and social assets that bind him to others".

Dr. Henry found that men and women with firm bonds of family, friends, and church had less than half the mortality rate of those without the comfort and balance of such ties. If these people had a supportive home, work, and social life, they stayed a lot healthier than those expressing dissatisfaction in their private and work lives. One group of physicians with established tendencies toward depression, anxiety, or anger was found by Dr. Henry to get sick at a much younger age than those with a calmer temperment.

The work of Dr. Henry and Dr. Hans Selye indicates that a sense of mastery over one's destiny is an essential asset for good physical and emotional health. When feelings of helplessness or insignificance set in, the neuroendocrine system in your body shifts into overdrive and disease is far more likely to occur.

It seems obvious from these and other research findings that your feelings affect your health. When rejection makes you angry, upset, and frustrated, you aren't able to cope with the stress that's placed on your body. Then you have to face difficulties like disease, serious illness, or even death.

When you look at all the problems rejection can cause, you might ask yourself why anyone in their right mind would seek acceptance in the first place. The answer to that question lies in understanding the forces that drive people to action. These forces are called wants, needs, and desires. They're described in the next section.

WANTS, NEEDS, AND DESIRES

There are two types of forces—positive and negative—that influence and sustain behavior. Positive forces are called wants, needs, and desires. They cause you to move toward objects, conditions, and people you're attracted to. Negative forces are called fears or aversions. They cause you to move away from things you don't like.

Wants, needs, and desires are terms that are often used interchangeably. They all represent a perceived deficiency, but the essential nature of the deficiency can vary considerably. Needs are generally thought to be more essential than wants or desires, although in many cases, the difference is merely semantic.

You respond not only to objects, conditions, and other people in your environment, but to yourself as well. You respond to your thoughts, emotions, and bodily needs. In doing so, you develop and understand your self-concept. As you mature, your self-concept becomes the nucleus around which your wants, needs, and desires are organized.

Your self-concept helps determine the particular kinds of needs you choose to pursue. You obviously won't go after all your needs at the same time. Whether you try to satisfy a particular need or not depends on your physiological condition, the situation you find yourself in, and your thoughts at the time the need is felt.

A noted psychologist by the name of Abraham Maslow suggested that a person's needs could be arranged in a hierarchy. He felt that as you began to satisfy your basic needs, you'd move on to needs that existed at a higher level of complexity and involvement with the self. His hierarchical list of needs is shown here.

1. **Physiological Needs:** hunger and thirst.
2. **Safety Needs:** security, order, and stability.
3. **Belongingness and Love Needs:** affection, identification, and affiliation.
4. **Esteem Needs:** prestige, success, self-respect, and achievement.
5. **Self-Actualization Needs:** self-fulfillment.
6. **Cognitive Needs:** knowledge.
7. **Aesthetic Needs:** beauty.

Maslow felt that once you were fed, you'd be off in search of interpersonal satisfaction. As the hierarchy indicates, you generally don't seek acceptance until after you feel secure within yourself.

Maslow's order of needs is directed toward total enhancement of the self. He felt that the needs in his list were basic to all human beings. But he also recognized that the desire to satisfy those needs could vary from person to person.

The things you want can be categorized in several ways, depending on who's looking at them and why. When you look for acceptance from someone, even if it's for economic reasons, you're trying to satisfy a social want. There are several social wants that are particularly important in rejection because of their impact on the development of your self-concept. Here are some of the major ones.

1. **Acquisition Want:** the desire to possess or hoard material possessions.
2. **Affiliation Want:** the desire to be associated with or in the presence of other people.
3. **Altruistic Want:** the desire to help others.
4. **Curiosity Want:** the desire to explore and investigate your environment, seek novel stimulation, and strive for knowledge.
5. **Power Want:** the desire to control other people or objects, to get their obedience, to compel their actions, and to determine their fate.
5. **Prestige Want:** the desire to be highly regarded by your associates.

These wants aren't arranged in any specific order. You move to satisfy them according to the way you feel about the world around you and the people you find in it. They're important to consider because the frustration of any or all of them can lead to feelings of rejection.

You usually take definite action to satisfy your wants, needs, and desires, especially those involving relationships with other people. But to do so involves an element of risk. Whether you decide to take the risk or not depends on how intense your needs are. When your need is great, you'll risk rejection and try to gain acceptance. When your need is weak, you'll stand pat. If you take the risk and your need is not satisfied, you'll face a potential loss of love, self-esteem, and injury to your pride. That's when your inability to satisfy your wants, needs, and desires can lead to frustration.

Now you're probably wondering what to do to protect yourself from the effects of frustration and negative stress. There are several things that might work for you, and they're all discussed in the next section.

DEFENSE AGAINST STRESS

The negative stress that's caused by rejection stems from your relationship with at least one other person. There are three defensive reactions you can use to combat this interpersonal stress:

1. You can physically, verbally, or otherwise attack the person who's causing your distress.
2. You can escape from the relationship without acknowledging the rejection or going on the attack.
3. You can ignore the person who's causing your distress and try to come to terms with your rejection.

The two overt defenses are attack and escape. When you attack, you take out your hostility and anger on the person who rejected you through various kinds of aggressive behavior. When you escape, you do everything you can to avoid the source of your anxiety.

In the third defensive reaction, you ignore the person who rejected you and try to put up with your situation as best you can. You resort to what psychologists call ego-defense mechanisms.

Ego-defense mechanisms are conscious and unconscious ways you use to protect your self-esteem from insult and injury. You also use them to restore your physical and psychological equilibrium.

Here are some of the more common ego-defense mechanisms you can use in response to being rejected.

Humor. You discover and recognize humor in the outlandish inconsistencies of your situation. When you get rejected, you laugh it off by finding something funny in the experience. You make a not-too-serious assessment of your qualifications and the criteria for acceptance. In recalling your rejection, you focus on some humorous aspect.

Altruism. You provide constructive and instinctively gratifying service to other people. You do this to compensate for the perceived lack of altruism you see in others, especially those who've rejected you. Sometimes you get so excessively altruistic that you totally disregard your own needs.

Sublimation. You convert unacceptable impulses into socially acceptable activities. You might take your hostility and anger out on the racquetball court or in some other strenuous activity like chopping wood. You feel that these activities are much better than physically attacking the source of your distress and anxiety.

Compensation. You make up for a perceived failure or weakness in one area by excelling in a different or related activity. If you've been rejected because of a physical handicap, you compensate by working extra hard in an area where physical abilities aren't necessary.

Rationalization. You justify deficiencies to yourself and others by making excuses or giving plausible and acceptable reasons for trying to be accepted. If you've been rejected because you couldn't meet a standard requirement, you'll de-emphasize the importance of being accepted. Or you'll justify your rejection by saying you couldn't get excited enough to make a serious try at being accepted.

Projection. You attribute your acknowledged feelings, faults, and deficiencies to others. You pass the buck to the one who rejected you or to anyone else who might be involved. Or you find fault with the selection system, process, or criteria. You lay the blame for your rejection anywhere but on yourself.

Repression. You keep undesireable impulses buried in your subconscious. You don't allow your inner feelings of rejection to reach the level of consciousness where they'd be obvious to others. By holding everything inside, you think you can protect your self-esteem and not act out irrational responses like anger, hostility, and frustration.

Almost everyone has used ego-defense mechanisms at one time or another to maintain self-esteem and reduce anxiety. They can be very effective in helping you reach compromise solutions to problems that involve your self-concept. Used positively, ego-defense mechanisms protect and enhance your self-esteem. Used negatively, they provide a means of escape from reality and an inappropriate defense against anxiety.

In a positive sense, ego-defense mechanisms protect against things that threaten the personal integrity and worth of your self-concept. They soften the realistic harshness of failure. They protect your self-concept from the ravages of anxiety. And they help you maintain an internal state of homeostasis so you can operate more effectively in a changing world.

Problems come up when ego-defense mechanisms interfere with the maintenance of your self-integrity instead of helping it. They sometimes lead to self-deception and reality distortion. They can also keep you from realistically coping with normal problems of social adjustment.

Ego defense mechanisms are not always subject to conscious checks and balances because they usually operate at subconscious levels. You'll be very upset whenever anyone else points out that you're using an ego-defense mechanism. Because once an ego-defense mechanism is brought up to the conscious level, it doesn't work very well. Without that protection, you have a hard time dealing with the source of your distress.

Up to this point, you've seen how feelings of rejection get started. You've also seen what you've been doing to yourself in the way of self-injurious behavior. And you've seen how that behavior can lead to serious mental and physical problems. You must also know by now that your self-concept plays a major role in the way you respond to rejection. You'll see just how important it is as you read through the next chapter.

THE CONCEPT OF SELF

The self is a hypothetical concept. It can't be weighed, measured, or handled, but enough research has been done to identify it as being the single most important element in the process of rejection.

Your thoughts and ideas about the self and its importance to you is called your self-concept. It's the image you have of yourself. It includes your character, personal interests, behavior, emotions, and attitudes as you know them.

This chapter introduces you to the concept of self. It also describes how your self-concept is involved in rejection. It explains what is meant by your extended self, inferred self, and true self. Finally, it offers some exercises you can do to enhance your self-concept.

INITIAL THOUGHTS

Psychologists see the self as something that manages the operation of your body. It makes you act in certain ways after it receives impressions from your environment. Psychologists also see the self as your point of reference for the past, present, and future. When psychologists study the self, they look at it as a factor of interpersonal relationships, or as an expression of personal values and goals.

Your self-concept is formed in part by the attitudes you hold. Your reality attitudes reflect your view of yourself and the world around you as you think they really are. Your ethical attitudes reflect your hopes for things as you'd like to have them be. Whenever you express these and other attitudes, people make inferences about you. They often come up with a notion of who and what you are.

On one hand, you have your own self-concept. On the other hand, you have the ideas that other people come up with. It's extremely important for you to keep them apart. If you can't separate your ideas from the ideas of others, you'll create a tremendous conflict between what you think your values, goals, and attitudes are, and someone else's idea of what they should be. You'll tear yourself apart psychologically if your self-concept can't override the one that other people expect of you.

The difference between your self-concept and someone else's idea is especially critical whenever you feel rejected. It wouldn't be at all unusual for you to look at yourself through the eyes of the person who rejected you. Many people do this to see where they might have failed to meet the other person's expectations. If you spend too much time doing this, you'll be unable to see yourself as you really are. You'll only have the perception—or misperception—of someone else to go by. Your weak self-concept will invariably cause you to be emotionally devastated whenever you're rejected.

If you have a strong self-concept, you'll also have a lot of self-confidence, self-satisfaction, and self-esteem. These feelings are determined more by your self-concept than by any kind of rejection, no matter how painful it might be. That's because the act of rejection has far less impact on how you feel about yourself than your self-concept does.

If your self-concept is healthy and strong, you're not likely to suffer feelings of rejection. You'll be disappointed at not being accepted, but you won't take it out on yourself through self-injurious behavior. If you have a weak self-concept, you're bound to experience a lot of psychological pain whenever you're rejected.

The relationship between your self-concept and the pain of rejection is illustrated below.

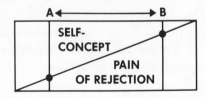

Point **A** represents a strong self-concept and weak feelings of rejection. Point **B** represents a weak self-concept and painful feelings of rejection. As your self-concept gets weaker, the pain of rejection increases. As your self-concept gets stronger, the pain of rejection decreases.

You can run into problems even when you have a strong self-concept. The problems come up when there's a difference between your perceptions of true self and ideal self. The ideal self is the one you'd like to become. The true self is what you really are. If the difference between them is small, clinical evidence suggests that you have an inflated and very shaky self-esteem, based on a blanket denial of most or all of your shortcomings. On the other hand, a large gap between the two indicates that you have a very low self-esteem. This relationship is illustrated below.

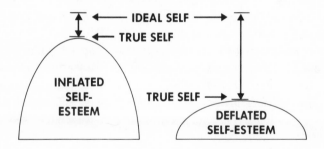

If your self-concept is weak, you probably lost some of your self-esteem when you were rejected. Now you have to strengthen your self-concept to get rid of your feelings of rejection. One way you can do this is to get a better understanding of how your self-concept is involved in the process of rejection.

In the acceptance/rejection process, people make decisions about you at two levels, depending on how involved they want to get. At both levels they come up with an idea of who they think you are. These two ideas, together with what you know about yourself, make up three aspects of your self-concept. They include your extended self, inferred self, and true self.

These three aspects of your self-concept are important in dealing with any rejection. After you get to know and understand them, you'll be able to direct your feelings of rejection to the aspect that can withstand the most pain. And as soon as you can control your psychological pain, you'll eliminate a lot of unhappy feelings.

YOUR EXTENDED SELF

Your extended self is the aspect of your self-concept that's most visible to other people. It's the grist of first impressions, but it's not the real you. It's only an extension of what you really are and know yourself to be.

If you look back through your lifetime, you won't find more than a dozen people who took the time and effort to really get to know you. You might include your parents, spouse, brothers and sisters, and one or two close friends. But even the people who are closest to you probably don't know everything about you.

Other people don't get as close as your friends do. They look at what you've done, what you have, and the way you act. They spend very little time in assessment and evaluation. Then they apply their own criteria in determining who they think you really are. This is the way most people react to you. They only see what's obvious.

Your extended self is rejected most often because that's what most people see. When the college admissions officer, personnel manager, customer, or book editor rejected you, they didn't have any more to go on than a brief glimpse of your extended self. Even if they got to know you fairly well, they wouldn't have rejected your true self because you didn't offer it.

There are at least six elements that make up your extended self. All of them affect the image you present to others. As you study each of them, you'll see that they're the parts of you that are out in front where they can be rejected most often. Here they are.

Affiliations. These are the associations, relationships, alliances, connections, or unions you've made with other objects or individuals in your environment. You can be a Republican, Democrat, Episcopalian, Baptist, union member, or anything else you've chosen to be identified with. Affiliations involve labels, and you can easily be rejected because of the labels you wear. This element of your extended self provides another clue to the dynamics of rejection. Many people make decisions that are based on prejudice, bias, predispositions, or favoritism. They react favorably to things they like, and they reject those they dislike. This should have nothing to do with your self-concept. But even if prejudice was involved in your rejection, you probably still suffered some loss of self-esteem.

Accomplishments. This element includes your achievements, exploits, deeds, acts, feats, skills, talents, gifts, proficiencies, capabilities, and creative expressions. You might have been rejected for a job you wanted because you didn't have the needed accomplishments or background. You might also have been rejected because you were overqualified.

Accomplishments can be rejected in a fair and honest way, or out of jealousy and spite. Your true self isn't involved, because that's not what you presented for acceptance. The only thing that's been evaluated is an extension of your true self.

You can also be rejected because of negative accomplishments like failures, blunders, and deficiencies.

Acquisitions. Most acquisitions consist of material possessions, but awards, recognitions, and status symbols can also be involved. You can be rejected for what you have or for what you don't have. And you can be accepted out of sycophancy or rejected because of jealousy. Social memberships are often determined by a person's acquisitions.

Acquisitions are highly regarded in modern society. They're often considered when rejections are made. But acquisitions shouldn't affect your self-concept. If you'd allow them to, you'd be in real trouble. You'd be just as shallow as the one who uses them as a selection criteria.

Altruism. This is the need to help others. But sometimes people just don't want to be helped. Sons and daughters often reject the well-intentioned interference of their parents. Many parents respond by feeling rejected. In most cases, it's the extended hand that's rejected, not the person it's attached to.

In a negative sense, you can be rejected if others think you lack altruistic feelings and are seen as egotistical, greedy, or covetous.

Power. If you appear to have a lot of power, you could be rejected out of fear. Those who reject you do so out of self-defense or for self-enhancement. In most cases, the rejection doesn't go beyond the appearance of being powerful. Your true self is seldom a part of the rejection process.

You can also be rejected if you appear weak, impotent, listless, or without any power at all.

Prestige. This element of your extended self reflects your status, glory, reputation, prominence, notability, or significance. You can be rejected for having too little prestige or too much. People who are held in high regard by their associates can be rejected as easily as a person of ill-repute. When prestige is involved, your rejection is based on the moral judgments or feelings of insecurity of the people who reject you. Again, your self-esteem should remain strong.

Your extended self can be rejected many times and for many different reasons. Here are some examples that might compare with some of the rejections you've experienced. In cases like these, there shouldn't be any psychological pain if your self-concept is strong.

1. You're a Minnesota Viking fan and you're rejected because of it.
2. You're rejected because you drive a foreign car.
3. You're rejected for membership in a social club because you live in the wrong neighborhood. Or you're accepted because you live in the right one.
4. You're rejected as a do-gooder.
5. You're rejected because you pose a real or imagined threat to someone else.

In each case, it's your extended self that's been rejected. Your true self should remain intact. You wouldn't have much substance if you thought you were a foreign car, a neighborhood, or a football team. You're much more than that. If you feel hurt when your extended self is rejected, then you must work hard to build up your self-esteem. If you don't, you'll continue to suffer the pain of rejection whenever people make superficial decisions about you. Every action taken against your extended self will be viewed by you as a rejection. You'll not only have more rejections, but they'll be more devastating because there'll be little or no strength in your extended self.

With a strong self-concept, you'll be able to withstand any and all rejections of your extended self. You'll even be able to change your extended self to fit the situation in which you're looking for acceptance, as long as it isn't a significant change and doesn't affect the integrity of your true self.

There's another aspect of your self-concept that's generated by other people after they've made a thorough analysis of who and what you are. It's your inferred self.

YOUR INFERRED SELF

Some people will go out of their way to get to know you. They'll study your characteristics and ways of behaving through direct observation, indirect examination, or scientific assessment. Then they'll make inferences about the things they see. And they'll come up with something called your inferred self.

Personality is another term for your inferred self. It's the most representative description anyone can make of you in a social setting. Your personality—or inferred self—differentiates you from everybody else. It can include such things as your disposition, temperament, individuality, distinctiveness, charm, personal attractiveness, outward character, and friendliness. It's everything someone else can see in you if they take the time to look.

Your inferred self is not often involved in the process of rejection. That's because few people take the time or make the effort to analyze, evaluate, and become sincerely interested in you. Many people won't do it even after you've invited them to accept or reject you.

You shouldn't get emotionally upset when you know your inferred self is the object of rejection. The other person rejected the results of their assessments, which may or may not represent the kind of person you really are. Even if their assessment is carefully done and well documented, it might not be accurate. You'll obviously be disappointed at not being accepted, but you shouldn't take it out on yourself by creating anxiety, depression, or negative stress.

Sometimes it's easy to become what other people see you as being. That saves a lot of introspection and difficult self-analysis on your part. It might even win you an acceptance or two. It's also very dangerous, because if others can create you by accepting what they see, they can also destroy you by rejecting it.

The one thing other people can't destroy is your true self. It's the most important thing you have going for you. And the more you know about it, the stronger you'll be.

YOUR TRUE SELF

Your true self is the real you. It's the way you think you really are and how you'd like to be. It's based on your ideas of right and wrong. It's a reflection of all your strengths and weaknesses. It helps you relate to everything and everyone around you. Your true self is the foundation for all your behavior. But it can only be described by you, because you're the only one who knows what it is.

You can do a simple test to see if you really know your true self. If rejection of any kind, by any person, causes all kinds of emotional problems for you, you don't have a very good concept of your true self. But if most rejections fail to bother you, then your concept of true self is pretty strong.

Some parts of your true self are hidden behind subconscious motives that act as barriers. These subconscious motives exist in your mind, but you're not immediately aware of them. Or if you know they exist, you might not be aware of how important they are to you. You have to break down these barriers before you can really get to know everything about your true self. That takes a lot of hard work, introspection, and a willingness to recognize and accept shortcomings.

Your subconscious motives are tied to your wants, needs, and desires. They have a significant impact on whether you're accepted or rejected. You might, for example, be applying for membership in an exclusive social club, trying to make a big sale, or hoping to win the affections of someone you admire. Your subconscious motives might be to satisfy your needs for affiliation, acquisition, or power, all of which relate to your extended self. If your motives are strong, then they're probably the only things that can be seen by the people you're dealing with.

These subconscious motives create barriers for you and for the one you hope will accept you. You can't see past the barriers to determine how your efforts will enhance or detract from your true self. The person who's evaluating you can't see past your superficial desires, because that's all you've given them. They certainly aren't going to take the time or make the effort to break down the barriers you've erected. In all likelihood, you'll end up being rejected without having a clear understanding of your true self.

To eliminate your feelings of rejection, you have to recognize the overwhelming nature of your subconscious motives for seeking membership, financial success, or affection. Then you have to get behind those motives to see why they exist. Once you've characterized them, you can remove them if you have to. You'll discover something about your true self in the process, and you'll become much stronger in doing so.

You don't have to open up your true self for all to see. It's a very private part of you that you won't readily reveal to other people. As you gain knowledge about your true self, you'll get stronger. And with added strength will come a willingness in interpersonal relationships to risk exposure of more and more of your true self.

Getting to know your true self might take some time. But with hard work and exercise, you should find it easy.

SOME EXERCISES

Think about the three aspects of your self-concept that have been presented in this chapter. Do you know what your true self consists of? Do you know what others see in you when they talk about your personality? Can you accurately describe your extended self; the one that creates first impressions?

If it's still a little hazy, it might help to go back and read the three sections over again. It might also help to consider the three concentric circles that are shown below. The outer circle represents your extended self. It's the one that everybody sees. The middle circle represents your inferred self. It's the one people see if they get closer and take the time to look. The inner circle represents your true self. You're the only one who really knows what it is, because you're the only one who can get that close.

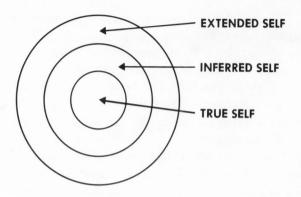

When you feel comfortable with the three concepts, think back to the rejections that caused you pain. Was the pain substantial and long lasting? Which element of your self-concept did you allow to bear the brunt of your feelings? Was your true self strong enough to withstand the emotional barrage you launched against it? Did you fend off the attack with your extended self? Did the people who rejected you attack you personally, or were they only reacting to the inferences they'd made about you?

Once you've developed a strong concept of your true self, you'll be able to withstand all rejections, no matter how painful they've been for you in the past. It might take some time, and it might not be easy at first. Here are some exercises that should help you get started.

Keep a Diary. Write down the things that make you happy and sad. Describe your feelings to things that happen in the world around you. Touch on things that reflect your values, ethics, and morals.

Develop a Profile. Write down characteristics you think best describe you. Include both strengths and weaknesses. If there's something that nobody else knows about, write that down too.

Create a Model. Identify people you admire and wish you could be like. Describe them as you would like to have yourself described using personal characteristics, values, and attitudes. Develop an ideal self-image that you can strive for.

Describe Rejections. Write down everything you can about each of your rejections. Tell what you did, what happened to you, and how you felt about it. For each experience, tell how it affected your self-concept.

Spend as much time as you can on these exercises. You'll get to know yourself a lot better, and your true self will be a lot stronger.

By now you should know how important your self-concept is. If it's weak, you're bound to suffer feelings of rejection. If it's strong, you'll be able to stand up against almost everything, even self-inflicted assaults.

You'll be in a much stronger position when you clearly understand the process of acceptance and rejection. The definition you found in the Introduction provides only a brief description of some of the things that can happen to you. As you read through the next chapter, you'll discover a lot more about this extraordinary phenomenon that's caused emotional havoc for you and many others.

THE DYNAMICS OF REJECTION

Rejection, in its simplest form, involves one person refusing the offer of another. It's usually more complex than that because of the emotions involved. To completely understand what's going on, you have to look closely at the things people do and then figure out the motives behind those actions. And sometimes you can be fooled by what you see.

You can follow all the proper procedures while trying to be accepted and then be devastated by the insensitivity of the person who rejects you. Or you can be involved in a situation where you're under a thinly veiled threat of rejection. You can also feel rejected in some relationships even when rejection hasn't happened.

All of these conditions are discussed in this chapter along with the feelings of depression that seem to be present in just about every case of rejection.

INSENSITIVITY

Scientific studies have shown that realistic and believable information in advance of rejection will help soften the shock and reduce the negative aftereffects. In some cases the information can consist of nothing more than a warning signal.

There no doubt have been times when you've had to endure painful feelings of rejection because the person who rejected you was too insensitive to give you any information. If you recognized their insensitivity, you probably developed intense feelings of hostility and frustration on top of your feelings of rejection. All in all, your reaction to the other person's insensitivity could've caused a lot of harmful distress.

In many of your relationships you probably didn't hear anything about your chances for acceptance until you discovered that you'd been rejected. Then, if you got any information at all, you had to dig it out yourself, read about it in an impersonal form letter, or get it second-hand.

You probably ran into most of your problems when you were looking for a job. That's because there seems to be a lot of insensitivity in the hiring process. But there doesn't have to be. If you'd been given information about the selection process at the time you applied for a job, and told of decisions as they were made during the evaluation period, your feelings of rejection would've been cut dramatically.

Many of the people who direct the selection process claim they have neither the time nor the resources to be concerned with the feelings of those they reject. That's hard to believe, because form letters can be personalized, and postage stamps are not prohibitively expensive. There are effective and inexpensive ways of providing information. If people who make the decisions say it can't be done in every case, then it's a lousy commentary on the way they feel about their fellow human beings.

You can avoid unpleasant feelings of rejection by dealing directly with the insensitivity of other people. When you're first involved in an acceptance/rejection situation, ask for as much information as you can get. Look especially for evaluation criteria and timetables. Use that information as a cushion against possible feelings of rejection that might come in the future.

If the other person won't give you the information you need, then you're dealing with a very insensitive person. If you can recognize this early in the process, you won't feel so bad when you're rejected. You won't harbor illusions of altruism when the risk of rejection is high.

It's bad enough to generate feelings of rejection by ignoring people. It's even worse to deliberately incite the fear of being rejected.

HAZING

Hazing is a form of intimidation that carries with it the implied threat of rejection. It has existed for years as an organized activity in college fraternities, social groups, and professional organizations. It also exists in an organized fashion throughout our society. The members, or other "in-people", subject prospective or new members to abusive, humiliating, or disagreeable banter, ridicule, work, or criticism before granting them full membership or acceptance. Hazing can occur spontaneously or as part of a well-organized activity.

The theory behind hazing seems clear. As long as the threat of rejection remains strong, final acceptance into membership will be valued much more than if hazing were not done. Those doing the hazing say there's no better way to instill loyalty and a sense of gratitude for being accepted into the organization.

If you're being hazed, and if you know you'll eventually be accepted, the threat to your self-esteem is insignificant. But if you see rejection as a likely outcome, hazing in any form can leave you with tremendous feelings of frustration, stress, and anxiety.

Hazing can also exist apart from the process of acceptance or rejection. In many cases it's practiced solely as a means of tormenting another person. It's just another expression of one person's inhumanity to another. Even when it's vigorously condemned, it manages to persist in some form or another.

Dr. Carl Rogers, an eminent American psychologist, once wrote a paper in which he denounced the hazing of graduate psychology students by their professors. He felt the faculty members were more intent on hazing their students than on welcoming them as future colleagues. Rogers compared graduate schools of psychology with schools of medicine, dentistry, and other professions where he found evidence of apprenticeship instead of academic hazing. His condemnation of hazing and his pleas for a collegial relationship were generally rejected by his professional colleagues who denied a problem existed. So the concern over hazing can exist even among well-educated people.

Efforts have been made for years to eliminate the practice of hazing in college fraternities. And yet, it seems that a tragic death or serious injury happens all too often from this barbaric practice.

If someone is hazing you, consider it for what it is; a veiled threat of rejection. You need to weigh the value of being accepted against the humiliation of being hazed. You should also assess the motives of the people who are hazing you to see if you really want to be associated with them.

Sometimes you can feel rejected when there's neither a threat of rejection nor anything that looks like it. Then your feelings are due to your interpretation of the relationship you're involved in. This situation is explained in the next section.

BALANCE THEORY

You can feel rejected even when nobody has rejected you. And you can suffer the same feelings of frustration, stress, and anxiety. This strange situation can be explained by the balance theory. It's a theory about the way people react to one another.

Theories are ideas that are offered as explanations for phenomena that can't otherwise be proven. They're good guesses for why things happen like they do. They're very useful in helping people understand their own behavior or the behavior of others. That's why the balance theory is presented here; so you can better understand how feelings of rejection get started.

No matter how close you are to someone, you can still go through some psychological turmoil in your relationship. Your feelings toward each other can change a lot, especially when the two of you hold different attitudes toward other people or objects in your environment. When you both like the same things, you usually get along all right. But when there are major differences in your attitudes, you can generate feelings of rejection even when rejection doesn't exist. You can also experience feelings of jealousy, suspicion, doubt, and anger.

Dr. Fritz Heider and several other psychologists developed the balance theory to explain how attitudes create interpersonal problems. According to the theory, a conflict gets started when your attitudes toward other people or objects don't match the attitudes of your friend. Your set of mutual beliefs, judgments, and perceptions will be out of balance, and your joint system of attitudes will be disrupted.

This imbalance can exist not only between friends, but also between salespeople and customers, employers and employees, writers and publishers, husbands and wives, or any other combination of people. It leads to feelings of rejection whenever one person looks for acceptance from another.

Here's an example of how the balance theory works. Consider a romantic relationship between John and Mary. John likes Mary, and Mary likes John. But Mary also likes a group of people that John doesn't like. John can't understand how Mary can like a group he dislikes, especially if she really likes him, which is what she says.

The imbalance in John and Mary's attitudes will put stress on their relationship, especially if their attitudes are very strong. As long as Mary is attracted toward the group that John dislikes, he'll think Mary is rejecting him, whether she is or not. If John has a weak self-concept, his feelings of rejection will be enormous.

Here's a schematic diagram of what John and Mary's relationship looks like according to the balance theory. Positive attitudes are represented by (+), negative attitudes by (–).

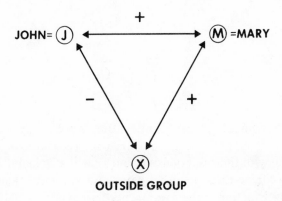

According to the theory, attitudes will be unbalanced when all three signs are negative (–), or when two are positive (+) and one is negative, as in the case with John and Mary. Over time, the attitudes will shift toward a state of balance in which all three signs will be positive or one sign will be positive and two will be negative.

The conflict between John and Mary creates stress that will continue to build as the need to resolve the conflict gets stronger. John's need for cognitive balance is frustrated, and he'll either get angry or jealous or both. His subsequent feelings of rejection will handicap his ability to resolve the conflict and remove the stress.

The conflict between John and Mary can be resolved in one of three ways, all of which will balance the system. First, John can change his attitude towards the group that Mary likes. If he got to know and like the group, he wouldn't be threatened by Mary's attraction to them. Second, Mary could develop negative attitudes toward the group for the same reasons that John already uses. Finally, John and Mary can change their feelings toward each other. Mary can still be attracted to the group, John can still dislike them, and they can proceed to dislike each other. This third option will probably happen if the conflict and stress they've introduced into their relationship is allowed to continue.

The three alternatives are schematically represented below.

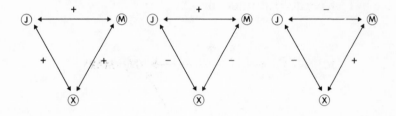

The resolution of interpersonal conflict is not always as simple as theories like this suggest. John and Mary will probably look for balance and consistency in their relationship, but they'll also look for solutions that will maximize their potential gains and minimize their potential losses. The satisfaction of their wants, needs, and desires plays a crucial role in the way they resolve their conflict.

The need John and Mary have for each other will be weighed against the need they have for acceptance or rejection of another attitude object. This need will be affected by the nature of the object and its importance to each of them. The object can be a person, a group of people, an organization, a political philosophy, a sexual preference, or anything else that John and Mary feel strongly about.

Feelings of rejection on the part of either John or Mary will develop from their conflict over opposing attitude objects. They can get rid of those feelings of rejection and reduce their conflict in an efficient and nonthreatening way. All they have to do is focus on the differences in their attitudes, judgments, and perceptions toward other objects. If they can resolve those differences, their feelings of rejection will disappear.

The example of John and Mary can be applied to other interpersonal relationships. A salesperson may lose a sale because of a conflict in attitudes. If the salesperson focused on the differences in attitudes, instead of feelings of rejection, the chances of making a sale would be much better.

You've seen how conflicts in attitudes can make people feel rejected. And whenever they feel rejected, they almost always feel depressed.

DEPRESSION

Depression is a common companion to feelings of rejection. It's a neurotic condition, characterized by dejection and despair, in which you take on a defeated or hopeless attitude toward the things that bother you. It's a normal, short-term response to an unhappy situation like a death in your family, marital problems, sexual dysfunctions, financial worries, or rejection. Events that are particularly susceptible to producing a depressive reaction are those that involve your health, physical appearance, bodily functions, social status, or relationships with other people.

Depression is generally brought on by a stressful event that involves a loss. You could lose someone you care for very much through death or divorce, or because they moved out of your area. Your loss could be even more personal, like losing your hair, your figure, or your youthful vigor. Since rejection is almost always seen as a loss, rather than a gain, depression is a natural outcome.

You'll encounter some serious mental problems if you allow your depression to become a long-term condition. That's why it's very important to recognize and acknowledge symptoms when they first appear. Just accepting the fact that you're depressed and wanting to do something about it is a giant step toward feeling better.

Unconscious hostility is a major factor in almost every depressive reaction. When you're depressed, you get mad at the person who rejected you. Then your hostility causes guilt feelings when you recognize that the other person isn't really the cause of your feelings of rejection. As soon as you see that, you turn your hostility against yourself. That's followed by feelings of unworthiness and despondency, along with more depression and hostility. A vicious cycle gets started that's hard to stop.

When you're depressed, you forget how to act when things start going your way. You fail to recognize even the slightest evidence of acceptance, and focus instead on how much pain and agony still remains from the last time you were rejected. When other people acknowledge your acceptance, you respond with more hostility, because you think your suffering is being ignored. Then you feel guilty again for being so hostile and your depression is off and running again.

If you're like most people, your depression will disappear when you no longer feel rejected. That doesn't necessarily mean you have to start being accepted more times than you're rejected. It means you have to get rid of your feelings of rejection any way you can. You can do it by recognizing that you'll never be totally immune from rejection. You can also do it by letting yourself feel good whenever you're accepted, even if it's for an insignificant event. And of course the key to getting rid of all your depression is to develop a strong and healthy self-concept.

You can do several other things to get rid of your feelings of depression. But first, you must recognize that the worst part about depression is the trapped feeling of not being able to do anything. You've got to overcome that feeling and keep active. Stop brooding and look for a change of pace in your life. Take one step at a time if you have to, but keep moving. Recognize and accept your limitations along with your strengths. Acknowledge the fact that you're not perfect. Then you won't be so critical of yourself.

Be flexible and have a wide variety of ways of getting pleasure out of life, especially when you're under stress. Treat other people as individuals; it'll help get rid of your hostility. Do helpful things for other people; it'll build up your self-confidence and break the hold of moodiness and inaction. Finally, do things that you can enjoy and have control over. Nothing breeds success more than the success you create through your own efforts.

> Sitting still and wishing
> Makes no person great.
> The Good Lord sends the fishing,
> But you must dig the bait.

You've been given just about all the information you need to understand the phenomenon of rejection. You know what it is and why it makes you feel the way you do. You know your feelings of rejection are self-inflicted. And you know the terrible effect they can have on your physical and mental well-being. So unless you're a masochist, you should be ready to get rid of those feelings and start feeling better again. You can survive your rejection, but you have to take some definite steps to do it. The next chapter will show you how.

HOW TO SURVIVE REJECTION

First of all, you have to accept the fact that your rejection is over and done with. There's nothing you can do now to change what has already happened. If you spend time worrying about it, you'll lose sight of the present and stumble into a cloudy future. You can't go back and make a new start, but you can start right now and make a brand new ending.

Resolve now to pick up the pieces and move ahead. Set some specific goals and objectives for yourself. Here are a few things to shoot for.

* Get rid of your feelings of anxiety and depression.
* Recognize that you're not alone in the world.
* Replace feelings of anger with feelings of love.
* Quit feeling guilty.
* Restore whatever you feel you've lost.
* Reinforce your self-esteem.
* Learn more about the process of acceptance/rejection.

There are three very important things you should *not* do, otherwise you'll wallow in self-pity the rest of your life. First, don't seek revenge against the one who rejected you. Second, don't punish yourself for seeking acceptance. And third, don't withdraw from social contact.

Now, go through and study each of the suggestions in this chapter. Decide which ones can help the most and get started on those right

45

away. Come back to the others when you have time, and see where they can help too.

Some of these suggestions might inspire you to come up with ideas of your own. As you think of them, write them down at the end of this chapter. Elaborate on them as best you can. Then incorporate them into your daily living wherever they can do the most help.

Keep track of your results in a diary and review your progress from time to time. You'll get rid of your feelings of rejection in no time at all if you really put your mind to it. Don't be discouraged if things don't happen right away. Keep up your enthusiasm, even when you encounter difficulties. Your diary will tell you how well you're doing.

The first suggestion is the key to all the rest. Take a look at it now. It'll help you in everything you do.

BE HAPPY

You won't be bothered by the customary aftereffects of rejection because you can't be happy and sad at the same time.

Take advantage of the great therapeutic qualities of happiness. It'll not only improve your state of mind, but it'll also get rid of the harmful side effects of rejection. Happiness can even save your life as Norman Cousins reported in his book, *Anatomy of an Illness.*

The importance of being happy was also recognized by Nobel Prize Laureate Albert Szent-Gyorgyi. He said, "Human activity is dominated by the search for happiness. Happiness is, in turn, essentially self-fulfillment; a state in which all needs, be they material or intellectual, are satisfied."

If you're like everybody else, you're motivated to look for happiness. But your rejection could've sidetracked you. Maybe you gave up on your quest for happiness, and now you're wallowing in the depths of despair. You don't have to feel that way. Because as Abraham Lincoln said, "You're about as happy as you make up your mind to be."

The choice is yours. You've got the power to control the way you're going to feel. Since you can't be happy and sad at the same time, one or the other will have to go. It might be hard to keep up a happy attitude in the face of rejection, but it sure beats feelings of frustration and anxiety. There are several things you can do to develop a happy outlook.

Start right now by thinking happy thoughts. Put anger and frustration out of your mind. Look for happiness all around you. Read happy books, go to happy movies, and laugh when you think something is funny. Develop a happy attitude and you'll find that everyone around you will be happy too. It'll make you feel better, and it'll increase your chances of being accepted in the future.

Remember that good humor is the health of the soul, sadness is its poison.

It takes discipline and hard work to control your feelings. You can make it a lot easier if you take the time to really get to know yourself.

KNOW YOURSELF

You'll gain the strength needed to withstand the emotional side effects of rejection.

You gain strength through knowledge. The more you know about yourself, the stronger you'll become, because your knowledge and strength will be turned inward. You'll know what's been rejected and what's been left intact. This alone will give you the strength you need to overcome your feelings of rejection.

Know as much as you can about yourself. Keep a diary and make notes of the things that please you as well as those that make you unhappy. Identify your strengths and weaknesses. Know what your true self is made up of. Compare it with the self that others see. Know where the differences exist and come up with reasons why you think they're there.

Know your extended self and compare it with what you know about your true self and inferred self. When you're rejected, find out which of your three concepts of self was considered. And while you're at it, understand your motives for acceptance. They'll tell you a lot about yourself.

The importance of knowing yourself has been expressed by many famous people over the ages. To "know thyself" was considered one of the great oracles of the Greeks. Here's what others have said.

Shakespeare: "Of all knowledge, the wise and good men seek to know themselves."

Johann Zimmerman: "Never lose sight of this important truth, that no man can be truly great until he has gained a knowledge of himself."

Novalis: "No one who has not a complete knowledge of himself will ever have a true understanding of another."

B. P. Warburton: "Of all exercises, there are none of so much importance or so immediately our concern, as those which let us into the knowledge of our own nature. Others may exercise the understanding or amuse the imagination; but these only can improve the heart and form the human mind to wisdom."

Speaking of exercises, you'll find an easy and efficient way of learning about yourself in the Appendix. You can use it to identify your strengths and weaknesses, your likes and dislikes, or anything else that helps describe you. It should give you a pretty good picture of who you are. Take some time and look at it now before you go into the rest of this chapter. Then come back here and find out how to stand up for your own cause.

STRENGTHEN YOUR EGO

You'll protect your self-esteem and turn away self-destructive thoughts.

Your self-esteem probably suffered a serious blow when you were rejected. Now you need to build up your ego so you can move forward with confidence and enthusiasm. A strong self-concept will help defend you against self-criticism and the real or imagined attacks of others.

Give yourself a pep talk and tell yourself why you're a good and capable person. Recognize your strengths where they exist and quit tearing yourself down. There's got to be a lot more good in you that you're willing to admit. But if you're like a lot of other people, you'll find it hard to give yourself the recognition you deserve.

Mark Twain said, "We can secure other people's approval if we do right and try hard. But our own approval is worth a hundred times more, and no way has been found of securing it."

This doesn't mean you should be egotistical. It just says that you should strengthen your ego by giving yourself credit where credit is due. You need a strong ego to cope with stress. And one of the major sources of stress is your dissatisfaction with life and disrespect for your own accomplishments.

Minimize any weaknesses you might have. Look at them objectively and make improvements wherever you can. Don't let your concern over a perceived weakness lower the respect you have for your strengths. If you see yourself as unacceptable and convey that feeling to others, they'll reject you. And the more you get rejected, the lower will be your self-esteem. You'll start a devastating cycle of self-rejection that'll be hard to stop.

One of the purest joys known to man or woman is the satisfaction that comes with a true and noble accomplishment. Be willing and able to accept that satisfaction and give yourself credit for being a good person. Recognize awards you've won. Accept praise when it's warranted, and thank people when they compliment you. You'll feel a lot better about yourself when the verdict you pass on your own behavior is confirmed by the people who know you.

As soon as you start feeling good about yourself, go back and figure out what happened to you when you were rejected.

UNDERSTAND THE PROCESS

You'll get rid of the misunderstanding that causes your anger, frustration, or other harmful feelings of rejection.

You've got to understand the process of being rejected if you want to get rid of the anxiety you feel. You need to know what you offered and what was rejected.

A lot of your frustration and anxiety could be due to the fact that you offered one thing and the other person rejected something else. This is especially important if you applied for and were turned down for a job. You might have been rejected because you didn't have the needed qualifications that were required by the person making the decision. If you're a salesperson, you might have offered to satisfy a need that wasn't expressed.

The person who turned you down undoubtedly rejected your extended self. Like most people, they probably didn't have the time or the inclination to thoroughly evaluate you and make inferences about your true self. So your self-concept and your self-esteem should still be intact.

Your offer was evaluated in terms of the wants, needs, and desires of the other person. You shouldn't be overly concerned about not being able to meet all those expectations. If you tried to be all things to all people, you'd lack substance and wouldn't have any personal integrity. Just do the best you can and accept occasional rejections as being inevitable.

When looking at the process of rejection, consider the objective factors that were acted upon along with the subjective feelings of the people who were making the decisions. Analyze everything you can, but pay particular attention to timing, procedures, and economic costs and benefits. If you know why you were rejected on one occasion, you'll know what to do to be accepted on the next. You'll not only reduce the frequency of rejections, but you'll be able to handle them much better when they do occur. And be realistic. Being turned down once doesn't mean you'll be turned down forever.

While you're looking at the process of rejection, be sure to consider the second-most important person involved; the one who rejected you.

THINK OF OTHERS

You'll develop a better understanding of your experience, and you'll get rid of your anxiety and self-pity.

The more you know about the process of rejection, the easier it'll be to get rid of those lousy feelings. You not only need to know what happened, you also need to know who did it and why. The people who reject you are every bit as important as you are. So look beyond your own pain and agony. Otherwise you'll only get half the picture.

The people who reject you can be just as insecure as you are when you make your offer. They're probably concerned about making a correct choice whether you're applying for a job, trying to sell them something, or hoping to establish a personal relationship. Their anxiety can even be much worse than yours, especially if someone else is looking over their shoulder to make sure they don't make a mistake.

The people whose acceptance you want might have been burned in the past. They might still remember the pain they felt when they made a wrong choice. They know they're vulnerable, especially when they have to make tough decisions. Because of that, they might be reluctant to start a new relationship with you. They won't reveal their true reasons for rejecting you because they don't want to get personally involved. They might already have lots of problems of their own that you don't know about. But just knowing that these problems exist should help you understand that you're not alone in the process of rejection.

Establish a relationship of mutual trust and understanding between you and the person who rejected you. Then both of you will be able to objectively assess what happened in your relationship. You'll be open in your exchange of information, without fearing reprisals of any kind. To reach that understanding, you have to have a good opinion of yourself and the other person.

You'll reap additional benefits when you become sincerely concerned with the joys and sorrows of someone else. You'll no longer be wrapped up in your own self-injurious tendencies. You'll lose your feelings of rejection and gain peace of mind as you share your knowledge of an emotional experience with the one who was in it with you.

You can't think objectively about another person if your emotions are all screwed up. So a first-order priority is to get rid of feelings that can distort your thinking.

AVOID HOSTILITY

You'll wipe out stress and tension and their harmful side effects.

Hostility is about as useless as throwing a rock at a hornet's nest. It's also a sign of emotional instability and immaturity. It's a byproduct of the frustration you feel over being rejected. The sooner you quit being hostile, the sooner you'll be able to get rid of your feelings of rejection.

Hostility can create dangerous amounts of stress. It can build up to the point where you feel you need to lash out at someone. If you express your hostility through devious or destructive behavior, you'll end up hurting yourself more than the person it's directed to.

On the other hand, if you supress your hostility and keep it from being expressed, it'll build to dangerous levels that can cause psychosomatic disorders or lingering depression. The best thing you can do to prevent hostile feelings is to not let them get started in the first place.

Hostility has a component of fear in it. When you're rejected, you get frustrated and think someone is trying to hurt you. Your fear of being hurt leads to feelings of hostility that are directed toward the person who did the rejecting. In order to get rid of your feelings of rejection and hostility, you have to get rid of your fears. You can do this by developing the courage to enter all kinds of relationships along with the peace of mind to not be frustrated if you're unsuccessful.

You suffer more from your feelings of hostility than from the things that made you mad in the first place. Allow your hostile feelings to continue, and you can almost guarantee that you'll be rejected again in the future. So forget your rejection and concentrate on doing something that will ensure the success of your next attempt.

Take the energy you spend on hostility and use it instead on productive thoughts. Be forgiving and tolerant and find out why you were rejected. See where your frustrations come from and attack the source. If you can keep from being frustrated, you'll eliminate your hostility. And if you get rid of your hostility, you'll get rid of stress and tension. Then, as your peace of mind is restored, your feelings of rejection will vanish.

Remember that you're about the same size as the things that make you mad.

Spend some time and get rid of the excess emotions that keep you from feeling better. Be prepared to make some discards.

DISREGARD THE REASONS WHY

You won't be hobbled by self-justification, self-punishment, or the need for revenge.

An objective analysis of your rejection will help you deal with the emotional aftereffects. It will also provide you with guidelines for future behavior. Just don't get obsessed with trying to find out *why* it happened and who's to blame. Otherwise you'll lose your objectivity. You'll spend all your time making excuses for yourself, punishing yourself, or trying to get even with the person who rejected you. You're frustrated because you were rejected and unable to reach a goal. If your frustration continues to grow, you'll try to justify your behavior, especially if you consider your rejection a personal failure. But if you spend all your time trying to come up with a plausible excuse for being rejected, you won't have time for anything else.

Excuses are nothing more than mental camouflage, a poor attempt at self-deception. They're ineffective ways of trying to protect your self-respect by proving that something unpleasant didn't really happen.

You can keep your self-respect without making excuses or rationalizing your behavior. Just be willing to accept your rejection as a learning experience and not as a sign of personal inadequacy. Profit from it by seeing what really happened. Analyze it objectively. Then take what you can from the experience and prepare for your next attempt.

You shouldn't punish yourself for being rejected if you gave it your best shot. If you gave less than that, then forget it. You can't turn back the clock and do it over again. Instead of saying, "I should have", be ready next time and say, "I will."

You have the choice. You can consider your rejection a sign of personal failure, or you can view it judgmentally as a learning experience. You can wail and gnash your teeth and punish yourself, or you can work to improve the nature and quality of future relationships. But if neither you nor anyone else can correct a complaint of yours, then don't complain—to them or to yourself.

The need for revenge can be just as damaging to you, because anything you do to hurt the one who rejected you will come back to harm you a hundred times more. Your time is far too valuable to waste on feelings of anxiety, anger, and hostility. You'll get a lot more done and feel better besides if you turn your attention to objective facts instead of subjective reasons. You'll learn more, and you'll greatly improve your chances of acceptance in the future.

One of the best ways to improve is to find out where you made a mistake. Take whatever information you can get and apply it where the need for improvement is greatest.

LOOK FOR FEEDBACK

You'll get rid of the anxiety that comes from uncertainty when you find out what really happened to you.

Get as much information as you can about your rejection. It'll help you evaluate your experience, correct your mistakes, and get rid of any misunderstandings you might have. It'll also make you feel much better, because most of your anxiety that comes from fear and misunderstanding of the unknown will be erased.

You'll also improve your chances of future acceptance if you can find out why you were rejected. Look for milestones and see where you stood along the way. Look for clues that will tell you when and why you were turned down. Then apply your knowledge to your next attempt at being accepted.

You've got to know what to ask for in order to get a clear picture of what happened. You also need to build up your self-esteem before you can start asking questions. If you're uncertain about who you are, you'll vacillate all over the place as you try to respond to the other person's critical judgments.

Compare your self-concept with the characteristics other people see in you. Notice any differences that exist and be prepared to reconcile them. But don't give up your integrity just to conform to the notions of others.

Find out from the people who rejected you what you need to do to improve your chances of acceptance in the future. Their suggestions can be very helpful if you'll accept their candid opinions. Don't be argumentative, and don't keep asking them if they still love you. You need to get as much objective information as you can, and you won't get it if you let your emotions get in the way. Consider using a questionnaire. It could be a lot less threatening for the other person than a face-to-face confrontation with you.

Know what to do with the feedback after you get it. Check the explanation you get against your own judgment. Be sensitive to valid information, but keep in mind that the people who reject you may be reluctant to reveal their true feelings for fear of offending you. Don't blame yourself for being rejected just because you can't get reliable information. Take what's offered, evaluate it, digest it, apply it where you can, and move on to your next experience.

The whole world is out there for you to look at. So don't restrict your view to the things that only happen to you. Broaden your horizons and look beyond your own self-interests.

LOOK AROUND YOU

You'll discover previously unknown ways of overcoming your feelings of rejection.

One of the best ways for getting rid of your feelings of rejection could be right in front of you. All you have to do is set aside your pain and agony and go looking for it. You'll find it among the techniques that other people use to overcome their feelings of rejection.

There are lots of other people who feel just as bad as you do and who are experiencing rejection that's every bit as painful as yours. But many of them are handling their rejection very well. It would help you tremendously if you could find out how they're doing it. You'd start to forget your problems as you tuned in on somebody else's. At the same time, you'd discover ways of handling your rejection that you wouldn't otherwise have known about.

Sometimes people will give you advice, even when you don't ask for it. Listen to what they have to say, even when you think they're intruding. You might get some ideas you never thought of before. Thank the people who offered their help. Consider their suggestions honestly and pursue them vigorously. Then after you've accepted or rejected their advice, tell them what you've decided and why. By being considerate instead of defensive, you'll make your life a lot easier and you'll learn more about rejection. You'll also win some new friends and keep the ones you already have.

There's another group of people you should listen to. They're the ones you've rejected. Find out how they feel. Learn what it's like to be on both sides of the fence. See if you've given them the same kind of information you look for in your own attempts at acceptance.

The Golden Rule—to do unto others as you would have others do unto you—is the keystone of interpersonal relationships. Give the people you reject the same consideration you expect from others. You'll make life a lot more enjoyable for both of you, because you can't sincerely help another without also helping yourself.

When you get to feeling that nobody has been treated as bad as you have, remember the words of Ferris Greenslet.

What evil luck soever
For me remains in store,
Tis sure much finer fellows
Have fared much worse before.

HANG IN THERE

You'll be so busy you won't have time to think about being rejected.

Perseverance is the perfect medicine for almost every emotional set-back. If you can carry on in spite of interference, opposition, or discouragement, your feelings of rejection will disappear. Your persistent efforts will keep you looking toward the future as disappointments fade rapidly into the past.

Move forward and learn as much as you can about what you're doing. You'll be better off than if you sat still and felt sorry for yourself. At the same time, you'll find out if you're doing the right thing or not.

If you know you're headed in the right direction, then keep at it. Remember that every important task seems impossible when you first try it. To be successful, you have to work hard, put up with setbacks and disappointments, and keep faith in what you're doing. Sometimes you have to reach down deep within yourself to come up with bulldog courage. But if your pursuit is worthwhile, you'll find what you need to continue in spite of your initial rejection.

If you discover that your task is hopeless, then back up, look for another opening, and pursue success in a different direction. Don't let your feelings of rejection dampen your enthusiasm or you'll never taste the fruits of success or reap the benefits of additional knowledge.

As you keep trying, you'll find that few things are impractical in themselves. When failure occurs, it's generally due to a lack of persistent application. If you stay with something long enough, and if it can be done at all, then you're bound to be successful. With each new success will come added strength to conquer your feelings of rejection.

If you have the right outlook, your successes will far outnumber your defeats. But inevitably you're going to run into a defeat you didn't expect. If you approach it in the right way, it won't even slow you down.

RECOGNIZE DEFEAT

You'll have a much better perspective of what's possible and what's not.

Sometimes there's nothing you can do but think of your rejection as a defeat. You shouldn't let that upset you, because defeat is a common, everyday occurrence. Neither fear it nor give it more significance than it deserves. Defeat is inevitable, but it's not insurmountable. It offers rich opportunities to learn and grow when it's approached with a positive point of view.

You'll develop deep-set feelings of resentment and bitterness if you refuse to accept defeat and are obstinate in your belief that you're right. You'll be much better off if you can muster the courage to admit you've failed. You'll avoid a lot of stress and tension, and your mind will be open to new and exciting challenges.

Look back on your rejection with an open mind. See where others kept you from being successful. Determine where a need was frustrated. Find out if there was something you could've done differently that might have enabled you to be successful.

Learn to bounce back and be resilient. Think of defeat as nothing but a temporary setback, the first step toward something better. If you're afraid of defeat and deny yourself the chance to fail, you'll never move ahead. You won't be hurt as often, but you won't enjoy the riches of success either. If, on the other hand, you're willing to accept some initial disappointments, you'll soon develop the ability to withstand defeat. You'll keep learning as you move toward the satisfaction of your goals and objectives.

The way you treat yourself is far more important than whether you won or lost. Sometimes it doesn't take much at all to make you feel a whole lot better.

REWARD YOURSELF

You'll be motivated to try again and again and again.

Give yourself credit for taking the initiative and assuming some risk instead of punishing yourself for being rejected. You'll be more realistic in your outlook and you won't be so hard on yourself.

Life isn't so simple that you can easily identify a single event that led to your rejection. It's a lot more complicated than that. Whatever you did to seek acceptance undoubtedly involved several steps, especially if it took quite a bit of time. You probably completed some of the steps successfully, and some you might have failed.

Examine your mistakes carefully, learn from them, and make improvements where needed. Then leave your mistakes behind. You'll just aggravate your feelings of rejection if you dwell on them or punish yourself for having made them.

Look instead at all the things you did right. Give yourself a reward for each one. It doesn't have to be anything fancy, just something that's important to you, makes you feel good, and motivates you to look for more success in the future. It can be a bottle of wine, a vacation trip, a night on the town, or some other special treat.

You might be a writer who's had a book or magazine article rejected. Look at all the steps you successfully completed before you sent your material off for publication. Give yourself credit for creating the main idea and turning it into a finished piece. Acknowledge your efforts at writing, editing, and producing. The next writing you do will be even better than the last if you focus on your accomplishments instead of your rejection.

Maybe you're a salesperson who's lost a big sale. If you look only at the things that caused your rejection, you won't see all the good things you did. Failure to see your strengths and abilities will lead to another rejection and another after that.

Your rejection might have involved an affair of the heart. Your feelings of rejection may be very painful and hard to endure. So look instead at all the good times you had. You found new places to see and things to do. You discovered things about yourself and your feelings you didn't know before. Consider those things as successes and reward yourself for doing them well. You'll be able to enter other relationships with positive feelings and be loved for it.

TRANSITION

Now is a good time to stop and think about what you've read so far. You've been introduced to twelve ideas on how to survive rejection. Some of them may have been new to you, and others you might have already known about. They should all make you think about the way you've been responding to rejection.

Before you go on to the next chapter, write down any ideas you have for surviving rejection that aren't listed here. Elaborate on them where you can. Then you'll know exactly what to do when you face rejection again.

Be sure to come back to this chapter anytime you think your feelings of rejection are getting the best of you. A periodic review will help keep you on the right track.

Now go on to the next chapter and find out how you can promote acceptance.

ADDITIONAL THINGS I CAN DO TO OVERCOME
MY FEELINGS OF REJECTION

1.

2.

3.

4.

5.

6.

7.

8.

HOW TO PROMOTE ACCEPTANCE

In the last chapter you learned how to deal with rejection after it happened. You were given suggestions that told you how to get rid of your feelings of rejection so you could start feeling good again. You were encouraged to look at the good things that happened to you and to put the bad things in their proper perspective.

This chapter deals with the future. It tells you how to avoid rejection and promote acceptance. It's closely related to the last chapter and builds on many of the earlier suggestions. It's based on the assumption that you've already experienced the pain of rejection and would like to have something better.

As you go through each of the suggestions, start applying the ones that will help you right away. Go back to the others when you have time and apply them wherever you can. If you come up with any new ideas, add them to the list at the end of the chapter.

The first thing you have to do to promote acceptance is to know what you're trying to accomplish.

ANALYZE YOUR SITUATION
You'll know what to pursue and what to avoid.

If your situation is worth getting into, it's worth knowing about. A thorough analysis will help promote acceptance even if the probability of rejection is high. With realistic and believable information, you'll know where you stand at all times. And you'll know where to turn when you're faced with minor frustrations.

Know what your chances are for being accepted and what alternatives are open to you if you're rejected. Unrealistic expectations are easily frustrated. If you don't know where to turn when you're turned down, you can expect feelings of resentment, anxiety, and depression.

Find out what the expectations are of the person who'll be accepting or rejecting you. Know the criteria that will be used and when it will be applied. Know when significant decisions will be made. Understand the process that will be used to notify you of any decisions. Know when and if you'll be able to offer additional information in your own behalf. Determine what appeal procedures are available. Your enthusiasm and interest in the process should generate a favorable response from the person who'll be evaluating you.

Deal directly with any fears you have about being rejected. Don't allow them to influence your understanding of the situation. Fears live in the dark corners and hidden recesses of your mind, but they wither and die when you drag them out into the open and meet them head on. Dale Carnegie offered this formula for conquering fear in his book, *How to Stop Worrying and Start Living.*

1. Ask yourself what's the worst that can possibly happen.
2. Write down precisely what you're worrying about.
3. Prepare to accept the worst if you have to.
4. Write down as many solutions to your problem as you can think of.
5. Decide on the best solution.
6. Start immediately to carry out that decision.
7. Calmly proceed to improve on what you see as the worst.

The words of Thomas Carlyle are also helpful in conquering your fears. "Our business is not to see what lies dimly at a distance, but to do what lies clearly at hand."

As you're gathering facts, be sure you know everything you can about yourself. Know what strengths and weaknesses you'll be bringing into your situation. Know what you'll be offering, and see if the other person does too. If rejection is a distinct possibility, know what will be rejected and what will be approved. An objective analysis will help prepare you for any eventualities that might occur. It will also help soften the shock and aftereffects in case you're rejected.

You can fall into a trap of believing the world will come to an end if you're rejected or that acceptance is the best thing that could ever happen to you. There's much more to life than the anticipated outcomes of individual experiences. You've got to analyze each situation as a unique element in a much larger picture.

You can get a very good picture of what you're trying to do if you can remember what has happened to you in the past.

REMEMBER YOUR PAST REJECTIONS

You'll learn to repeat the things that brought you success.

Events of the past will not only help you understand the present, they'll also provide guidance for the future. They'll give you a historical perspective of the events that led to your rejection. Build on the successful ones and avoid those that caused problems.

Analyze each one of your past rejections as thoroughly and objectively as you can. Talk about them with a close friend or someone else who really understands you. Once you're able to deal with your past rejections without falling apart, you'll be all set to take on new risks.

You can profit from your rejections if you don't fear them. Failures are inevitable, but they're not insurmountable. Handle them correctly and you'll improve your chances of being accepted in the future.

You can waste a lot of time second-guessing yourself. So don't dwell on the past by rehashing all the things you could've done or you'll be emotionally bankrupt. Find out what you did and learn from it. Then move into the present and prepare for the future. Drop the words "if only" when you're thinking about your rejections and replace them with "next time".

Find something humorous in your past rejections no matter how outlandish that might seem. Laughter cures many problems, and finding humor in a seemingly disastrous affair will probably help more than anything else to promote acceptance in the future.

Above all, remember that you're a good person. You don't have to compromise your self-respect for anyone.

KEEP YOUR SELF-RESPECT

You'll convince others that you deserve to be accepted.

Have a high regard for yourself as a genuine, worthwhile human being, and others will too. Their respect and admiration will almost always be translated into acceptance.

Whenever you enter a relationship with another person, you risk your self-respect for the gratification of personal desires. If you lose your self-respect, the destructive consequences will far outlast and outweigh any gratification you could possibly receive.

The fear of rejection and the need to conform can exert tremendous stress on your value system. The stress will be particularly difficult if you try to conform to another person's values and system of beliefs just to gain acceptance. This is especially true if the two of you are far apart to start with.

Trust yourself enough to enter a relationship. But also trust yourself to disengage from the relationship if it's not equal. Don't degrade yourself just to win approval. If other people try to manipulate you with a promise of acceptance, tell them to knock it off. You don't have to compromise your values or ethics for anyone.

Don't bend over backwards to be accepted. And don't give unnecessary favors to others, hoping that somewhere in the future they'll accept rather than reject you. You'll end up resenting yourself as much as the one who got you to do it. If you want to do something for someone, do it for the intrinsic pleasure it gives you, not for some hoped-for payoff.

Don't let approval-seeking become an insatiable need, or you'll end up feeling inferior and inadequate. You'll lose the insight you need for realistic self-perceptions. Thinking for yourself will become a terrifying experience, especially if you need someone else's approval to survive.

You can maintain your self-respect by doing the best you can in spite of what others expect from you. This is especially true when you're under pressure to conform. That doesn't mean blind pursuit of your own self-interests, but instead an adherence to well-defined goals and objectives with a concern for high ethical standards.

Abraham Lincoln lived an exemplary life by doing what he thought was right. He said, "If I were to read, much less answer, all the attacks made on me, this shop might as well be closed for any other business. I do the very best I know how—the very best I can; and I mean to keep on doing so until the end. If the end brings me out right, then what is said against me won't matter. If the end brings me out wrong, then ten angels swearing I was right would make no difference."

Lincoln knew he could be wrong, but by using his good judgment and doing the best he could, he kept his self-respect. He gained the love and admiration of millions while he did it. His life serves as an excellent model for anyone who must deal with the acceptance and rejection of others.

Lincoln also knew where his strengths were. If he had any weaknesses, he didn't put them out in front where they could get picked to pieces.

KNOW WHAT HURTS

You'll relate better to other people by avoiding things that cause emotional pain.

Know when you're psychologically vulnerable to being rejected so you can avoid situations in which you feel insecure, unprepared, or exposed to pain. Stay in safe territory where you're secure and nonthreatened. Build up your strength and wipe out your vulnerability to pain. When you're strong enough to enter new relationships, you'll be able to try for acceptance without the fear of getting hurt.

Make a list of areas in which you're most sensitive to rejection. Identify significant people in each area, especially those you want most to accept you. Here are some areas for you to consider.

* Love Relationships; involving spouse, parents, siblings, children, or friends.
* Work Relationships; involving supervisors, co-workers, subordinates, customers, or potential employers.
* Social Relationships; involving friends, neighbors, or club-members.

Determine the psychological consequences of being rejected by the people who mean the most to you. Recognize the things that make you angry and hostile. See what causes stress and tension. Then write down everything you can about the things that hurt, no matter how painful it is to do so. When you're able to do that, you'll be able to eliminate the troublesome ones with little or no difficulty.

By now you know that some experiences will be unpleasant. You have to decide how much pain you're willing to tolerate and how your tolerance is going to affect your chances of being accepted. There's no sense in being afraid of the things you know are going to happen. All you can do is make the best of a bad situation. At the same time, you shouldn't sit on your hands when there's still a chance of preventing a real disaster.

Learn as much as you can about the things that hurt you, and you've taken a giant step toward finding ways to avoid them. You still won't be accepted every time, but you'll avoid the hurt you previously felt when you were rejected.

Put criticism in its proper perspective if it hurts you. True criticism consists of neither praise nor blame. It serves only to discriminate between subjective judgments of good and bad.

Your weaknesses give strength to criticism that's unjustified. Allow others to wreak havoc on your feelings, and you'll have no one to blame but yourself. But if you can bear the weight of criticism, you'll find that it can help you. If you're strong and the judgment is fair, you'll learn from the criticism and grow stronger because of it. If the criticism is inappropriate, you'll discard it without letting it hurt you.

Sometimes you need added protection against the things that hurt you most. You need a good blanket of insulation.

INSULATE YOURSELF

You'll be immune to feelings of rejection and you'll develop an attitude that will be highly regarded by others.

The attitudes and outlook you present to other people will affect their decisions of whether to accept or reject you. If you think you're going to be rejected, you probably will be. But if you develop a positive mental attitude, you'll have a much better chance of being accepted.

A positive outlook on life helps insulate you from feelings of rejection. It offers psychological immunity against frustration, anger, hostility, and depression. It's all done in the way you look at life's experiences.

Work hard on your ability to endure the kind of pain and disappointment you've been vulnerable to in the past. Keep negative thoughts from taking control of your emotions and behavior. Recognize them for what they are, and don't let them influence your self-concept. Stand up against the things you fear. You'll be a much stronger person if you can see your world as a nonthreatening place to be.

Separate what other people say, think, and do from your own ideas of self-worth. Don't allow their rejection of you to disrupt your emotions. No one should have that much control over your peace of mind.

Maintain a positive attitude about yourself and the things you do, and don't let outside influences tear you down. And while you're at it, make a sincere effort to not be frustrated.

AVOID FRUSTRATIONS

You'll be accepted more often if you pursue outcomes that are attainable and within your reach.

There are two things you can do right away to promote your acceptance and avoid the frustration that comes from being rejected. First of all, choose goals and objectives that are realistic and attainable. Second, avoid insurmountable barriers.

Know what you can and cannot do. Take the time to analyze your strengths and weaknesses. Identify specific outcomes that you really want. Gear yourself up for those you're willing to work for. Pursue those that are within your reach. Disregard goals and objectives that seem impossible, otherwise you'll bring on failure and frustration.

At the same time, keep your dreams and aspirations alive. You can get just as frustrated by failing to live up to your potential. Balance your wants, needs, and desires with facts and reality. Then give it your best shot and take what comes. If you do your homework well, you'll approach your experience with confidence and enthusiasm. This alone will improve your chances of being accepted.

You can also avoid frustration by reducing the number and intensity of your wants, needs, and desires. If you try to get approval for everything, you'll set yourself up for rejection. Your insatiable appetite for self-gratification will distort your perception of reality, and you'll fail to strive for the things you really need. If you're consumed by your efforts to win approval, you'll spend all your time going to the mailbox or sitting by the telephone in anticipation of words of acceptance. You won't have time for anything else.

Frustration can also be avoided by knowing what kind of barriers you face and where they exist. You've probably seen some of them before in previous experiences. Be aware of them, and look for a way around them before you get too close. There are some barriers you just can't foresee, but you'll reduce their numbers considerably if you analyze your situation carefully and consider every possible outcome. And since you could be facing a variety of psychological, physical, economic, or cultural barriers, you're going to have to come up with a variety of strategies for identifying and getting around them.

As you move ahead toward new experiences, remember the philosophy of the turtle. You never get ahead unless you stick your neck out.

TAKE RISKS

You'll be welcomed as one who's not afraid of entering new and different relationships.

If you want to fulfill your potential, get the most out of life, and be accepted by others, you have to take risks, gamble, and possess the courage to fail. You might be able to avoid the pain of rejection without these qualities, but you'll never enjoy the pleasure of having a close, personal relationship with another person.

You'll always face the possibility of disappointment in any personal contact. You should still reach out, not just once, but several times, even though you know you'll be taking the chance of being rejected with each encounter. If only one person in a hundred says "yes" to you, that's a lot better than letting a hundred pass by in silence. It'll take a lot of discipline and courage to approach people the first time, but like every other task, it gets progressively easier when you do it over and over again.

Approach other people simultaneously, entirely on your own, without asking anybody else if you should or not. Feel free to give up a part of yourself in each experience. Giving involves risk taking because the possibility of being rejected is always there. But the benefits far outweigh the risks.

Giving benefits you and the recipient, and there are lots of things you can give. Some of them may be rejected, but many more will be accepted. Your personal gain will be fantastic.

Here's a list of things you can give to others.

* forgiveness to an enemy.
* tolerance to an opponent.
* love to a friend.
* a good example to a child.
* respect to your parents.
* respect to yourself.
* charity, benevolence, goodwill, and love to those who are in need.
* a smile to everyone.

You'll develop feelings of goodwill, gratitude, and trust when you enter into new relationships with other people. You'll share with those people your wish for a happy life. But all this could be lost if your fear of rejection keeps you from taking any risks.

Your success at taking risks will be greatly enhanced if you can balance your needs against the demands of others.

BE FLEXIBLE

Your ability to adapt to new situations and meet the changing expectations of other people will always keep you in demand.

Flexibility is the only thing that can insure your survival. Without it, you'd literally cease to exist. It's the key to homeostasis and resistence to stress. It makes life possible no matter how traumatic things seems to be.

You can get very uptight when you try to avoid anticipated feelings of rejection. You'll oversimplify your situation and try to put everything in nice, neat compartments. By tying everything up in tight little knots, you'll think you're secure. You'll actually be making things much worse than they really are.

You need to be flexible, not rigid. You must adapt to other people. groups, and goals. You have to change attitudes, shift strategies, or make whatever other adjustments are necessary to protect your well-being, promote acceptance, and avoid the feelings of rejection. If your initial perception of a relationship is wrong, you have to redefine it. You have to shift to other relationships if established ones are disrupted by the possibility of rejection. You must tolerate ambiguity and internal conflict, and you have to be willing to suspend judgment, especially on yourself.

You must be especially flexible in the commitments you make to other people. You don't ever want to get caught in the position of saying you'll feel a particular way forever just to gain acceptance. When you inevitably break that promise, for whatever reason, you'll suffer feelings of guilt, self-recrimination, and depression. Feelings change, and the decisions you make in response to those feelings also change.

Insist on the human right to be able to change your mind. This isn't a sign of weakness. It's a sign of a flexible human being who constantly receives information, assembles and reassembles it, and acts accordingly. You're not doing justice to yourself or to the other person if you rigidly adhere to a promise just to gain acceptance.

You've got to be flexible whenever you're actively involved with other people. Part of that flexibility comes from your ability to function in a variety of social situations.

CULTIVATE YOUR SOCIAL SKILLS

Your ability to handle yourself in a variety of social situations will make you a more acceptable person.

The way you interact with other people will have a definite impact on whether you're accepted or rejected. You'll have many more successes than failures if you're friendly and pleasant and can handle yourself in different social settings. That shouldn't require an overhaul of your social skills. You can get excellent results by working on just a few of them.

Learn to listen and ask intelligent questions. You don't have to agree or disagree with everything that's said, just acknowledge it. Don't interrupt other people or give instant advice. You'll be a skilled listener when you can listen with interest to things you know all about, even when they're told by a person who knows nothing about them.

You should also be a skilled observer of other people, especially of those who are socially adept. Find out as much as you can about them. See what they're doing that you're not. Make notes, then incorporate their skills into your own behavior.

You don't have to sacrifice your self-respect to be kind, polite, and sincerely interested in other people. And it shouldn't hurt you to want to be like other people who are more capable in social situations than you are. You can stay with your own attractions and improve on them whenever possible, but you should learn new skills in areas where you're lacking.

Avoid criticism, especially if you feel hurt when others criticize you. You must know how bad it makes you feel, so don't pass those bad feelings on to others. If you have a sincere desire to improve someone else, just remember that they might like themselves the way they are.

Have patience. You can't solve all the problems of social interaction in a week. Take time to learn. Practice your skills with everyone you meet. See what reactions you get. Pay particular attention to the things that please other people. But don't ignore the things that turn them off.

You can't polish your social skills in isolation. To really be at ease with other people, you have to reach out and touch someone.

TAKE THE INITIATIVE

Your offer of friendly companionship will make it easier for other people to accept you.

There's no better way of gaining acceptance than to establish warm and friendly personal contact with someone else. That's the best way other people have for assessing the value and sincerity of your advances. You don't have to establish an intimate relationship, and you don't have to worry about trying to measure up to someone else's expectations. Just be yourself and offer yourself in friendship to another person.

This might be hard for you to do if you see it involving an element of risk. It only involves risk if you let it. You have nothing to lose by just being a friendlier person. If a relationship doesn't work out, feel free to walk away from it. You can't get hurt that way.

You can establish friendly, first-name relationships with your grocer, banker, druggist, or anyone else with whom you come in regular contact. Concentrate on the things that attracted you to them in the first place. Find out what it is that they enjoy in you. Then, as you gain skill in building friendships, work toward developing deeper relationships.

Most people want to love and be loved in return. There's no risk in that, it's just plain happiness. If you offer friendliness, kindness, and a happy heart to someone else, you'll be welcomed with open arms.

Whatever you gain by extending yourself to other individuals will be multiplied many times over when you get involved with groups of people.

GET INVOLVED WITH GROUPS

You'll increase the number of people who'll be willing to accept you.

You can improve your chances of being accepted by getting involved with identifiable groups of people. You'll get rid of your fear of being alone, because you'll be around people with whom you share common interests. You'll communicate with people who understand you. By communicating your grief, you'll have less. By communicating your joy, you'll have more.

Group activities will multiply the benefits of individual contact as you get to know more and more people in the group. You'll learn what others expect in interpersonal relationships. That will help you relate with anybody, whether they're in or out of the group.

You'll learn to hold back many of your wants, needs, and desires for the good of the group. Your selfishness will fade away as you recognize the wants, needs, and desires of others. You'll discover that the secret of getting along with other people is to be considerate of their views and tolerant of your own.

You'll increase your chances of being accepted, because you'll increase the number of people who'll know you. Every group member you know will in turn know lots of other people who will be outside the group. Your chances of being accepted will increase tremendously because of the potential number of contacts you'll develop through your group activities.

The interests, needs, and goals of your group will establish common grounds for acceptance by the members. You won't have to search for ways of breaking the ice. The other members will identify with you even before they get to know you.

You can also increase your chances of acceptance by observing the other members of your group. See how they manage to be accepted. Recognize their strong points and incorporate successful strategies into your own behavior.

The more you work at promoting acceptance, the more successful you'll be. That means practice.

PRACTICE REJECTIONS

You'll be able to deal more effectively with other people because you'll discover what your strengths and weaknesses are.

This might sound like hitting yourself on the head with a hammer to see how good it feels when you stop. It doesn't have to be that painful. And it can be very effective in promoting acceptance.

Start practicing in areas that don't involve a lot of emotions. Ask to have lunch, get a cup of coffee, or go to a movie with someone you know will reject you. When the rejection comes, you'll probably experience some disappointment even if the chance of being accepted was remote. It's important to capture your response. So write down as many things about the event as you can. Record your feelings and make note of the reasons given by the other person for not accepting you. Pay particular attention to the effect rejection has on your self-esteem. You should write these things down every time you're rejected, whether you instigate it or not. Otherwise you might forget what's happened to you and fail to learn from it.

Your feelings of anxiety that come with rejection are probably due to your inability to make sense out of the process. So that means you need to practice more and be more observant. Look objectively at all the steps that were taken. See if you could've done something differently. Analyze the response you got from the person who rejected you. Find out if they were really doing what you thought they were doing to you. Take a close look at your feelings and try to see why you have them.

You'll feel a lot stronger as soon as you know what causes your feelings of rejection. You'll know what to expect and how to cope with it. By practicing rejection you'll discover where your emotional strengths and weaknesses lie. Through trial and error, you'll learn which responses are most effective in reducing your feelings of rejection. As you continue to practice on situations that aren't emotionally charged, you'll get much better at dealing with those that cause you serious amounts of distress. You'll discover things you didn't know about that can cause rejection and bring on feelings of anxiety and despair. Face those things head-on and eliminate them wherever possible. The self-confidence you'll gain will be evident to other people. They in turn will be more inclined to accept you in the future.

Now it's time again to look back at what you've read. You've just been given twelve suggestions for promoting acceptance. Examine them closely and add to them wherever you can. The more ideas you have, the better will be your chances of success. But don't just think about them, write them down here in this book. You'll remember them better and you'll be more inclined to carry them out.

The next chapter wraps up all the material you've found in this book. Hopefully, it'll send you off with good feelings toward a much happier life in the future.

ADDITIONAL THINGS I CAN DO TO PROMOTE ACCEPTANCE

1.

2.

3.

4.

5.

6.

7.

8.

IN A NUTSHELL

Now that you've read through this book, you should know what rejection is, how it happens, the feelings it can create, and the problems it can lead to. You should also know how to survive rejection and restore your equilibrium. And you should know how to promote acceptance so you can move forward toward a happy and promising future.

The most important thing you can learn from this book is that your feelings of rejection are far more troublesome than the situations that caused them. You're responsible for those feelings. You create them, allow them to grow, turn them against yourself, and then suffer the consequences.

Your defense against those feelings is pretty simple. Develop a strong self-concept and you won't allow them to get started in the first place.

All you have to do now is put your knowledge to work. Sift through everything you've learned here and come up with a plan of action. Decide what needs to be done and when you're going to do it. Then put your plan into action and leave those crummy feelings of rejection behind.

APPENDIX

To really get to know yourself, you have to identify the things that best describe you. Then you have to validate your discovery by applying your knowledge to a variety of social situations. It's a continuous process because you're constantly growing and changing as you go through life.

Here's a simple and easy way of finding out about yourself. It involves a procedure that's been described extensively in the book, *What Color is My Parachute?* You compare things you know about yourself to find out which are most significant for you. You identify the elements and the criteria for making the comparisons, so it's all self-directed.

The key to the procedure is a prioritizing grid that's shown on the following page. You can use the grid over and over again. Just copy it as it appears here. You can make it larger or smaller by adding or subtracting the elements you want to compare.

To start the process, identify four or five clusters of character traits you think best describe you. The procedure works best when you have at least ten, but not more than twelve items in each cluster. List traits that you think you have or that other people have identified in you. Here are four clusters and examples of traits for each one.

1. *Knowledge:* subjects that you know something about like mathematics, psychology, sociology, accounting, management, grammar, music, art, or literature.
2. *Accomplishments:* specific things you've done in your lifetime that you're proud of and that took initiative and imagination on your part.
3. *Specific Skills:* things you can do fairly well like cooking, woodworking, hunting, skiing, singing, writing, or painting.
4. *Personality Traits:* things that you or others have recognized in you like a sense of humor, seriousness, punctuality, perseverance, compassion, warmth, and sensibility.

79

PRIORITIZING GRID

1 2

1 3   2 3

1 4   2 4   3 4

1 5   2 5   3 5   4 5

1 6   2 6   3 6   4 6   5 6

1 7   2 7   3 7   4 7   5 7   6 7

1 8   2 8   3 8   4 8   5 8   6 8   7 8

1 9   2 9   3 9   4 9   5 9   6 9   7 9   8 9

1 10   2 10   3 10   4 10   5 10   6 10   7 10   8 10   9 10

CIRCLE COUNT

1 __   2 __3 __4 __5 __6 __7 __8 __9 __10 __
Total times each number got circled.

Number each item in your clusters from one through however many you have. Then look at the prioritizing grid. On the first line you'll see a **1** and a **2**. Compare item **1** in one of your clusters with item **2** according to the criteria you select. Decide which item you know more about, are strongest in, or enjoy the most. Circle that choice and go on to the next line where you see **1** and **3** and **2** and **3**. Again, with each pair, choose the item that stands out according to your criteria. Keep working through the grid until you've compared each item in your cluster with every other item.

Be sure you apply your criteria uniformly to each pair within a cluster. If you want, you can go back through the cluster another time and make comparisons with different criteria. But don't mix up your comparisons. Use the same criteria each time you work through the prioritizing grid.

After you've made your comparisons, count up the number of times each number was circled. Enter these totals in the spaces that appear right below the grid. Then recopy your list, starting with the item that has the most circles.

In case of a tie, where two numbers have the same number of circles, go back to the grid and see which one was circled when you compared the two of them.

You now have a list of things that you know something about, or like to be involved with. The one you favor most is at the top with the least favored at the bottom. This tells you something about yourself that you may not have known, or at least looked at in this way.

Go through your other clusters. Apply each list of items to the prioritizing grid like you did with the first cluster. You'll come up with four or five cluster lists that highlight your strongest points. You'll have one item you think is most important, followed by several others of decreasing importance.

You can go one step further and create a general inventory of all your strongest traits. Take two or three items from the top of each cluster and start another list. Work that list through the prioritizing grid like you did before. When you compare the items, circle those you think are most characteristic of you.

After you've gone through the grid, rearrange the items so the one with the most circles is on top. It may be a knowledge trait, a skill, or whatever, but something about that item is very important to you. Try to identify the reason for its importance, because it will help you discover more about your true self.

You can use the prioritizing grid in several ways to identify the lationship those things have for each other. You might make a list of people you'd most likely turn to in case of an emergency. Or you can rank order your experiences; those that brought you pleasure and those that caused you pain. You might even ask a close friend to go through your group of clusters to see how someone else looks at your traits.

Use the grid every way you can. If you work with it long enough, you'll come up with a pretty good description of who and what you are.

BIBLIOGRAPHY

Benson, Dr. Herbert. *The Relaxation Response.* New York: William Morrow and Company, Inc., 1975.

Bliss, Edwin C. *Getting Things Done: The ABC's of Time Management.* New York: Bantam Books, Inc., 1976.

Bolles, Richard Nelson. *What Color is Your Parachute?.* Berkeley: Ten Speed Press, 1981.

Carnegie, Dale. *How to Win Friends and Influence People.* New York: Simon and Schuster, 1936.

Carnegie, Dale. *How to Stop Worrying and Start Living.* New York: Simon and Schuster, 1948.

Coleman, James C. *Abnormal Psychology and Modern Life.* Chicago: Scott, Foresman, and Company, 1956.

Dyer, Dr. Wayne W. *Your Erroneous Zones.* New York: Funk & Wagnalls, 1976.

Friedman, Meyer and Rosenman, Ray. *Type A Behavior and Your Heart.* New York: Fawcett Crest Books, 1974.

Heider, Fritz. *The Psychology of Interpersonal Relations.* New York: John Wiley & Sons, Inc., 1958.

Kisker, George W. *The Disorganized Personality.* New York: McGraw-Hill Book Company, Inc., 1964.

Krantzler, Mel. "Rejection In Love", *Harper's Bazaar,* April, 1978. p. 113

Krech, David; Crutchfield, Richard S.; and Ballachey, Egerton L. *Individual In Society.* New York: McGraw-Hill Book Company, Inc., 1962.

Marks, Judi. "Rejection: How to Handle It", *Teen,* October, 1978. p. 18

Michelmore, Peter. "How Emotions Rule Our Health", *Reader's Digest,* October, 1981. pp. 39-45

Pellegrino, Victoria. "Rejection on the Job", *Harper's Bazaar,* April, 1978. p. 113

Proctor, Richard C. "On Depression, The Common Cold of Mental Illness", *Executive Health,* December, 1979.

Rubin, Dr. Theodore I. *Compassion and Self-Hate.* New York: David McKay Company, Inc., 1975.

Selye, Hans. *Stress Without Distress.* New York: J. B. Lippincott Company, 1974.

Shepard, Martin. *The Do-It-Yourself Psychotherapy Book.* New York: P. H. Widen, 1973.

White, Dr. Wendell. *The Psychology of Dealing With People.* New York: The Macmillan Company, 1937.

INDEX

acceptance: 3
  chances of: 73
  definition of: 3
accomplishments: 27
acquisitions: 27
advice from others: 55
affiliations: 26-27
altruism: 21, 27
  and insensitivity: 36
anger: 12, 17, 20, 21
  and stress: 17
analysis, value of: 61-62
anxiety: 2, 6, 14, 15, 21, 73-74
  and feelings of rejection: 1
  and hazing: 37
approval seeking: 64
attack: 20
attitude objects: 40
attitudes
  and balance theory: 38-41
  and feelings of rejection: 38
  conflicts in: 38-41
  ethical: 23
  positive: 67
autonomic nervous system: 15-16

balance theory: 38-41
  and attitudes: 38-41
  and feelings of rejection: 39, 40, 41
barriers: 13, 30-31, 67, 68

character traits: 79-81

commitments to others: 70
compensation: 21
concept of self: 23-33
conform, need to: 64
consequences of rejection: 13
Cousins, Norman: 62
Carlyle, Thomas: 62
conflict, interpersonal: 40
criticism: 66, 71

defeat: 57
depression: 41-43
  and feelings of rejection: 1, 42
  and hostility: 41-42, 52
  defined: 41
  eliminating: 42
diary: 32, 46, 47
distress: 14, 15

ego-defense mechanisms: 20-22
  and self-esteem: 20, 21
ego strengthening: 48-49
embarrassment: 10, 14
equilibrium: 14, 15, 20
escape: 6, 20, 21
evaluation: 3
excuses: 10, 21, 53
exercises: 31-32
extended self, 26-29
  rejection of: 29

failures: 63

85

fear
  and hostility: 52
  dealing with: 62, 67
  of being left alone: 2, 72
  of the unknown: 2
feedback: 54
feelings of rejection: 2, 6-11, 12, 17, 77
  and anxiety and depression: 1
  and balance theory: 39, 40, 41
  and guilt: 2
  and self-concept: 12
  and self-esteem: 25
  anticipated: 69-70
  flexibility: 69, 70
  frustration: 13, 15, 17, 19, 21
  and hazing: 37
  and insensitivity: 35
  and stress: 13-14, 17
  avoiding: 67-68

giving: 69
goals and objectives: 11, 67
Golden Rule: 55
Greenslet, Ferris: 56
guilt: 10, 14, 15
  and depression: 42
  and feelings of rejection: 2
  and negative stress: 14-15
group contacts: 72

happiness
  therapeutic qualities of: 46
  to survive rejection: 46-47
hazing: 36-38
  and anxiety: 37
Heider, Fritz: 38
Henry, James P.: 16, 17
hierarchy of needs: 18-19
hostility: 6, 15, 20, 21
  and depression: 41-42, 52
  and fear: 52
  and insensitivity: 35
  and stress: 51
  avoiding: 51, 52
hiring process: 36
humor: 21, 63

ideal self and self-esteem: 25

immunity
  from feelings of rejection: 66-67
  from rejection: 3
inferred self: 29-30
information
  ahead of time: 62
  and insensitivity: 35-36
  as feedback: 54-55
insensitivity: 35-36
  and altruism: 36
  and hostility: 35
  and information: 35-36
interpersonal stress: 14-15
interpersonal relationships: 23, 71-72

knowledge of self: 31-33, 47-48, 79-82

Lincoln, Abraham: 46, 64-65
listening: 55, 70-71

Maslow, Abraham: 18, 19

need to conform: 64
needs, hierarchy of: 18-19
negative stress: 14, 15
  and guilt: 14, 15
  effects of: 15, 16
Novalis: 48

other people
  who are rejected: 55
  who reject: 50-51

pain, psychological: 2, 65-66
  and self-concept: 24-25
past, importance of the: 63
personality: 29
perseverance: 56
physical problems: 15-17
positive stress: 14
power: 28
practicing rejection: 73-74
prestige: 28
prioritizing grid: 79-82
projection: 21
psychological pain: 2, 65-66

rationalization: 21

rejection
    definition of: 2-3
    practicing: 73-74
    reasons for: 52
    understanding process of: 49-50
relationships, significant: 65
repression: 21
revenge: 45
    need for: 52, 53
rewards, value of: 38
risk: 19, 68, 69, 72
Rogers, Carl: 37

second-guessing: 63
self-abandonment: 7
self-abuse: 7
self-accusation: 8
self-annihilation: 8
self-betrayal: 8
self-concept: 6, 8, 12, 18, 23, 77
    and feelings of rejection: 12
    and psychological pain: 24-25
    development of: 18
self-condemnation: 8
self-criticism: 8
self-deception: 8-9
self-defeat: 9
self-denial: 9
self-despair: 9
self-destruction: 9
self-doubt: 9-10
self-effacement: 10
self-esteem: 2, 6, 73
    and ego-defense mechanisms: 20, 21
    and feelings of rejection: 25
    and true and ideal self: 25
self-fulfilling prophecy: 9
self-gratification: 68
self-humiliation: 10
self-inflicted wounds: 6-11
    effects of: 12
    reasons for: 7
self-integrity: 22

self-justification: 10, 52, 53
self-pity: 10
self-punishment: 10-11, 45, 52, 53
self-renunciation: 11
self-repression: 11
self-respect: 64, 65, 71
self-righteousness: 11
Selye, Hans: 14, 15
Shakespeare: 47
social contacts: 45
social skills: 70-71
social wants: 19
stress: 2, 13
    and anger: 17
    and hostility: 51
    balance theory and: 38, 39
    defense against: 20
    definition of: 14
    frustration and: 13-14
    interpersonal: 14-15, 38
    negative: 14, 15-16
    positive: 14
    provoking events: 15
    response to: 15-17
subconscious: 21, 22
    motives: 30-31
sublimation: 21
suicide: 9, 14
synopsis: 3-4
Szent-Gyorgyi, Albert: 46

theories, definition of: 38
true self: 25, 30-31
    and self-esteem: 25
    est of: 30
Twain, Mark: 48
typical behavior: 5, 6

wants, social: 19
wants, needs, and desires: 18-20, 67-68, 72
Warburton, B. P.: 48

Zimmerman, Johann: 48